PSYCHOLOGY OF EMOTIONS, MOTIVATIONS AND ACTIONS

PSYCHOLOGY OF HATE

PSYCHOLOGY OF EMOTIONS, MOTIVATIONS AND ACTIONS

Psychology of Aggression
James P. Morgan (Editor)
2004. ISBN 1-59454-136-1

New Research on the Psychology of Fear
Paul L. Gower (Editor)
2005. ISBN: 1-59454-334-8

Impulsivity: Causes, Control and Disorders
George H. Lassiter (Editor)
2009. ISBN: 978-60741-951-8

Handbook of Stress: Causes, Effects and Control
Pascal Heidenreich and Isidor Prüter (Editors)
2009. ISBN: 978-1-60741-858-0

Handbook of Aggressive Behavior Research
Caitriona Quin and Scott Tawse (Editors)
2009. ISBN: 978-1-60741-583-1
2009. ISBN: 978-1-61668-572-0 (E-book)

The Psychology of Pessimism
Daniel X. Choi; Ravi B. DeSilva and John R. T. Monson
2010. ISBN: 978-1-60876-802-8

Psychological Well-Being
Ingrid E. Wells (Editor)
2010. ISBN: 978-1-61668-180-7
2010. ISBN: 978-1-61668-804-2 (E-book)

Psychology of Denial
Sofía K. Ogden and Ashley D. Biebers (Editors)
2010. ISBN: 978-1-61668-094-7

Psychology of Neuroticism and Shame
Raymond G. Jackson (Editor)
2010. ISBN: 978-1-60876-870-7

Psychology of Hate
Carol T. Lockhardt (Editor)
2010. ISBN: 978-1-61668-050-3

Bio-Psycho-Social Perspectives on Interpersonal Violence
Martha Frías-Armenta and Victor Corral-Verdigp (Editors)
2010. ISBN: 978-1-61668-159-3

Psychology of Risk Perception
Joana G. Lavino and Rasmus B. Neumann (Editors)
2010. ISBN: 978-1-60876-960-5

Psychology of Persuasion
Janos Csapó and Andor Magyar (Editors)
2010. ISBN: 978-1-60876-590-4

Psychology of Happiness
Anna Mäkinen and Paul Hájek (Editors)
2010. ISBN: 978-1-60876-555-3

Personal Strivings as a Predictor of Emotional Intelligence
Ferenc Margitics and Zsuzsa Pauwlik
2010. ISBN: 978-1-60876-620-8

Psychology of Thinking
David A. Contreras (Editor)
2010. ISBN: 978-1-61668-934-6
2010. ISBN: 978-1-61728-029-0 (E-book)

PSYCHOLOGY OF EMOTIONS, MOTIVATIONS AND ACTIONS

PSYCHOLOGY OF HATE

CAROL T. LOCKHARDT
EDITOR

Nova Science Publishers, Inc.
New York

NOTICE TO THE READER

The Publisher has taken reasonable care in the preparation of this book, but makes no expressed or implied warranty of any kind and assumes no responsibility for any errors or omissions. No liability is assumed for incidental or consequential damages in connection with or arising out of information contained in this book. The Publisher shall not be liable for any special, consequential, or exemplary damages resulting, in whole or in part, from the readers' use of, or reliance upon, this material. Any parts of this book based on government reports are so indicated and copyright is claimed for those parts to the extent applicable to compilations of such works.

Independent verification should be sought for any data, advice or recommendations contained in this book. In addition, no responsibility is assumed by the publisher for any injury and/or damage to persons or property arising from any methods, products, instructions, ideas or otherwise contained in this publication.

This publication is designed to provide accurate and authoritative information with regard to the subject matter covered herein. It is sold with the clear understanding that the Publisher is not engaged in rendering legal or any other professional services. If legal or any other expert assistance is required, the services of a competent person should be sought. FROM A DECLARATION OF PARTICIPANTS JOINTLY ADOPTED BY A COMMITTEE OF THE AMERICAN BAR ASSOCIATION AND A COMMITTEE OF PUBLISHERS.

LIBRARY OF CONGRESS CATALOGING-IN-PUBLICATION DATA
Psychology of hate / editor, Carol T. Lockhardt.
   p. cm.
 Includes index.
 ISBN 978-1-61668-050-3 (hardcover)
 1. Hate. 2. Hate crimes. 3. Hostility (Psychology) I. Lockhardt, Carol
T.
 BF575.H3.P76 2009
 152.4--dc22
                    2009054145

Published by Nova Science Publishers, Inc. ✦ *New York*

CONTENTS

Preface   **vii**

Chapter 1   Gender-Motivated Bias Crimes: Examining Why
                Situational Variables are Important in the Labeling
                of Hate Crimes   **1**
                H. Colleen Sinclair and Jordan T. Hertl

Chapter 2   Toward a Psychological Construct of Enmity   **35**
                Christopher R. Jones and Chris Loersch

Chapter 3   Hate, Revenge and Forgiveness: A Healthy,
                Ego-Strengthening Alternative to the Experience
                of Offense   **59**
                Patrick F. Cioni

Chapter 4   Do You Hate Me? Have I Hurt You?: Defenses against
                Growth, Separation, and Individuation That Create
                Interpretive Enactments Part One: Fender Benders and
                the Shared Defensive Systems of Less Difficult Patients   **83**
                Robert Waska

Chapter 5   Do You Hate Me? Have I Hurt You?: Defenses against
                Growth, Separation, and Individuation That Create
                Interpretive Enactments Part Two: Pit Stops and the
                Shared Defensive Systems of More Difficult Patients   **103**
                Robert Waska

Chapter 6   Hate and Love Scripts – Common Elements   **121**
                Barbara Gawda

Chapter 7   Hate: No Choice Agent Simulations   **137**
                 *Krzysztof Kułakowski, Małgorzata J. Krawczyk
                 and Przemysław Gawroński*

Index   **159**

PREFACE

Hate seems to be an emotion that won't go away. It is seen in the interactions between humans on a daily basis - on television, on the streets and in conversations around the world. 'Psychology of Hate' presents original analyses of hate from different perspectives including its manifestations in crime and personal relations.

Chapter 1 - Prototype theory (Harris et al., 2004; Inman & Baron, 1996) states that people have certain expectations when it comes to perpetrators and victims of acts of discrimination. The present study applied prototype theory to examine which variables affect the application of the label "bias crime." To examine the factors that affect hate crime labeling, a scenario was developed wherein victim type, severity of assault, assault location, and victim-perpetrator relationship were systematically varied. The likelihood that the participants would perceive bias as a motive and the labeling of the scenario as a hate crime were significantly affected by the independent variables. When it came to victim type, scenarios featuring an African-American victim were more likely to be labeled as a hate crime than those targeting a non-minority woman. Other factors that resulted in an increased likelihood of the application of the hate crime label were 1) the attack was committed by a stranger (instead of an acquaintance), 2) the attack was more severe (i.e., aggravated instead of simple assault), and 3) the attack occurred following a political meeting (e.g., NAACP, NOW) instead of occurring after a college class.

Chapter 2 - This chapter addresses a phenomenon pertinent to interpersonal hate: enmity. The authors first review the existing literature relevant to enemies, including a discussion of the relative neglect of this topic and the paucity of research on "the dark side of relationships." The remainder of the chapter addresses definitional, theoretical, and methodological issues in studying enmity.

In particular, the authors provide a novel construct definition of interpersonal enmity in which an enemy is a person someone dislikes; believes is malevolent or threatening; and wishes some degree of social, psychological, or physical harm upon. The benefits of this approach over other conceptualizations are discussed, as are multiple unresolved issues in conceptualizing enmity. The remainder of the chapter discusses future directions for research on enemy relationships including different classes or types of enemies, the integration of enemies with the self, the influence of enmity on person perception, and the role of individual differences in the development of enemy relations. Finally, the authors argue for the need to move beyond questionnaire and interview methodologies and discuss the benefits which can be obtained by more rigorous hypothesis testing and experimental design in this research area.

Chapter 3 - Forgiveness is a choice, a process and an internal response that involves release of negative affect including anger which, when chronic, can develop into hatred. It is not forgetting or condoning, and it does not necessarily lead to reconciliation though that is potentiated. The process of forgiveness includes 1) re-constructuring cognitions about the offender and self and 2) re-imaging the offender and re-experiencing self and violator. This object transformation results in ego development since objects and object constellations are the building blocks of ego identity (Kernberg, 1984). The ego is empowered to more effectively deal with conflict and associated negative affect due to abatement of anger and decreased internal arousal. This increases the ego's ability for effective communication and conflict resolution.

Stages of forgiveness and gradated cognitions typical of each stage are identified. Each forgiveness stage includes increasingly efficacious cognitions which exemplify a process of cognitive upleveling and ego strengthening. The distinction between forgiveness and reconciliation is important. Forgiveness is an intrapersonal event or process which potentiates but does not necessitate a behavioral coming together, while reconciliation is interpersonal and involves a behavioral encounter. Reconciliation involves risk-taking behavior which can become less threatening to the individual with increasing forgiveness and growing ego strength.

Chapter 4 - All patients struggle with psychological conflicts regarding love, hate, and knowledge. Some patients are troubled by phantasies of causing hurt and hatred in the object as a result of their quest for separation, individuation, and personal creativity. Success, ambition, differentiation, growth, change, and personal difference are all seen as creating, injury, unhappiness, anger, hatred, and rejection in the object. Therefore, these patients create intense and rigid defensive patterns of submissive, subordinate, and passive relating to prevent these internal catastrophes. These defensive mechanisms are mobilized through projective identification and create frequent patterns of interpretive enactments and counter-transference acting out.

This paper will highlight these vexing and humbling patterns of interpretive acting out we often find ourselves in as we try to reach out to patients but barely find a foothold before they slip away or before we lose our own therapeutic balance. Case material will be used for illustration to specifically examine how the defensive avoidance of certain wishes, feelings, and secret needs become part of the counter-transference and influence or pervert the interpretive process. As a result, the analyst may indeed be making helpful and accurate interpretations while also missing out on the more core aspects of the patient's in the moment phantasy and internal conflict. Theoretical and clinical material will be used to examine this phenomenon.

Chapter 5 - Some more disturbed patients in psychoanalytic treatment are struggling with primitive depressive anxieties and conflicts regarding separation and individuation. They feel obligated to follow what they believe their object needs, wants, or demands while at the same time feeling restricted and wanting to oppose or reject those needs for their own ambitions and choices. However, the phantasy of rejection and punishment as well as lasting harm to their object results in great conflict and a sense of entrapment. So, the patient is left with feeling they will create hate and harm if they admit their own needs, differences, accomplishments. Thus, these differentiation and individuation states are cloaked and camouflaged. While working with such patients, the analyst frequently is subject to projective identification attacks in which the patient's defenses against change, growth, separation, and individual choice become acted out in the interpretive field. Two cases are used for illustration and the need for careful counter-transference monitoring is discussed.

Chapter 6 - The presented research explains the common traits of affective scripts of hate and love and examines their mysterious nearness. We propose that this nearness is connected to common elements of mental representations of these feelings. The text first describes the script conceptions, the scripts theories concerning love and hate, and the theories that explain their nearness. The authors analyzed 180 stories about love and 180 stories about hate from the same group of people. These participants were of the same age, intellect, and educational level. The aspects of content and structure of scripts were compared. We concentrated on Schank and Abelson's conception of script elements: partner (positive/negative characteristics and emotions), actions (away from others/towards others), actor (positive/negative emotions), and story's type of ending (positive/negative). We used a multidimensional scaling method, Proxscal, to show the two scripts' common area.

Chapter 7 - The authors report our recent simulations on the social processes which -- in our opinion -- lie at the bottom of hate. First simulation deals with the so-called Heider balance where initial purely random preferences split the community into two mutually hostile groups. Second simulation shows that once these groups are formed, the cooperation between them is going to fail. Third simulation provides a numerical illustration of the process of biased learning; the model indicates that lack of objective information is a barrier to new information. Fourth simulation shows that in the presence of a strong conflict between communities hate is unavoidable.

In: Psychology of Hate
Editors: Carol T. Lockhardt, pp.1-34

Chapter 1

GENDER-MOTIVATED BIAS CRIMES: EXAMINING WHY SITUATIONAL VARIABLES ARE IMPORTANT IN THE LABELING OF HATE CRIMES

H. Colleen Sinclair and Jordan T. Hertl[*]
Mississippi State University, Department of Psychology,
Social Science Research Center, Mississippi State, MS, USA

ABSTRACT

Prototype theory (Harris et al., 2004; Inman & Baron, 1996) states that people have certain expectations when it comes to perpetrators and victims of acts of discrimination. The present study applied prototype theory to examine which variables affect the application of the label "bias crime." To examine the factors that affect hate crime labeling, a scenario was developed wherein victim type, severity of assault, assault location, and victim-perpetrator relationship were systematically varied. The likelihood that the participants would perceive bias as a motive and the labeling of the scenario as a hate crime were significantly affected by the independent variables. When it came to victim type, scenarios featuring an African-American victim were more likely to be labeled as a hate crime than those targeting a non-minority woman. Other factors that resulted in an increased likelihood of the

---

[*] Corresponding author: E-mail: csinclair@ssrc.msstate.edu

application of the hate crime label were 1) the attack was committed by a stranger (instead of an acquaintance), 2) the attack was more severe (i.e., aggravated instead of simple assault), and 3) the attack occurred following a political meeting (e.g., NAACP, NOW) instead of occurring after a college class.

INTRODUCTION

In 1989, Marc Lepine entered a University of Montreal lecture hall and forced the men out of the classroom. With just the women remaining, Lepine began to execute them one by one. After shooting each of the women, Lepine continued onto other areas in the building, killing a grand total of fourteen women before killing himself. In Lepine's suicide note, he blamed feminists for the problems in his life. The note also contained a hit list of prominent women in the community (Came, Burke, Ferzoco, O'Farreli, & Wallace, 1989).

Lepine's killing spree came to be known as the "Montreal Massacre" and it led to Canadian lawmakers advocating for the inclusion of "gender" in their anti-bias crime legislation, as few disputed that there could be a clearer example of a gender-motivated hate crime. However, rarely is gender-motivated hate crime so readily labeled. Most of the time, the role of bias in crimes targeting people based on gender is not so easily identified by the general public or legal decision makers (McPhail & DiNitto, 2006; Saucier, Brown, Mitchell, & Cawman, 2006). The aim of the present research is to examine a variety of variables that affect the application of the label "bias crime," and, through the manipulation of different aspects of a crime (e.g., victim-perpetrator demographics), determine which factors have more impact on labeling.

IDENTIFYING BIAS CRIMES

Although there are instances when a gender-based attack is labeled as a hate crime, as illustrated above, it does not happen very often (McPhail & DiNitto, 2006; Saucier, et al., 2006). Synonymous with the term "bias crime," statutes generally define a hate crime as a criminal act (e.g., assault, vandalism) perpetrated against a group or individual targeted, in whole or in part, because of their actual or perceived association with certain protected groups. Typically, the recognized protected groups are those identified by race, religion, ethnicity, or national origin, and, to some extent, sexual orientation. In fact, hate crimes as defined by the Hate Crime Statistics Act of 1990 are crimes which "manifest prejudice based on race, religion, sexual orientation, or ethnicity." Until the July 2009 passing of the Matthew Shepard Act (officially called the Local Law Enforcement Hate Crimes Prevention Act), gender was not included in the federal definition, and the majority of state anti-hate crime laws do not include gender. Further, even when gender is included in state laws, prosecutions are rare (see McPhail, 2002 for review). Legal agents still struggle with the application, as shown by McPhail and DiNitto (2002). Despite Texas law including "gender" in its hate crime statutes, McPhail and DiNitto found that Texas prosecutors were ill-informed about gender-bias crimes. Many were not aware of the inclusion of gender and struggled to conceive of an incident that would warrant the label of "gender-motivated" hate crime. Most of the attorneys interviewed (60%) did not believe that gender should be a protected class for hate crimes.

Identifying the Bias behind the Crime

A possible explanation for why people have difficulty in recognizing gender-bias hate crimes can be found by applying the research done by Inman and Baron (1996). To explore perceptions of race and gender discrimination, Inman and Baron proposed prototype theory. Prototype theory states that people have certain expectations when it comes to perpetrators and victims of acts of discrimination. The expectations that people hold determine the judgments that people make about what qualifies as acts of discrimination. Because hate crimes represent an extreme type of discrimination – namely *discriminatory violence* – it is possible that prototype theory is applicable to understanding when people see the bias underlying a crime. Few dispute that incidents like the Montreal Massacre, the Jonesboro school shooting, or other related incidents are a *violent* crime; rather, the dispute lies with whether it was a *bias-motivated*, and thus, discriminatory crime.

Inman and Baron's (1996) theory identifies the following factors as important to identifying discrimination. Their model points out that people have long-standing schemas regarding what they will or will not perceive as an act of discrimination. For example, a member of the majority making a decision to not hire a minority would be more likely to be labeled as discrimination than the opposite. This majority-minority distinction was one of the prototypical characteristics Inman and Baron suggested as instrumental to individuals' conceptions - and thus labeling - of discriminatory acts.

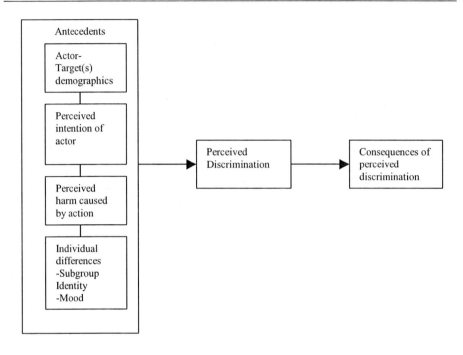

Figure 1. Harris et al.'s (2004) Prototype Model

Harris, Lievens, and Hoye (2004) adapted Inman and Baron's (1996) prototype model and identified specific categories that they felt best captured the factors that individuals use to interpret acts of potential bias in the workplace. In particular, three situational variables they found to be important in the labeling of discrimination were 1) victim-perpetrator demographics (or manager-employee demographics in their original model), 2) perceived intention of the perpetrator, and 3) level of perceived harm (Please see Figure 1). The resulting prototype was that if the situation featured a person in a power position who intended to discriminate and, in so doing, caused harm to the target, then this situation was more likely to be perceived as discrimination.

The Prototype of a Hate Crime

Just as prototypes exist for conceptions of workplace discrimination, so do prototypes exist for discriminatory violence. For example, Boyd, Berk, and Hamner (1996) found that police officers' conceptions of a hate crime were that it was a rare occurrence, typically a violent attack accompanied by slurs, often perpetrated by known hate groups (e.g., the KKK) against a stranger. The prototypical elements that the police identified fit into the categories of victim-perpetrator demographics (e.g., member of hate group, stranger), harm (e.g., violent attack as opposed to vandalism), and intent (e.g., perpetrated by individuals with a known history of committing intentionally hateful acts, attack accompanied by a group-specific derogatory insult). Craig and Waldo (1996) also investigated what individuals thought constituted a hate crime. Participants in their study believed that hate crimes were violent acts more likely to be committed against a member of a minority group by a White male. Craig and Waldo's (1996) study illustrates that, in addition to perpetrator demographics (e.g., white male, member of the majority), victim demographics were also important. Perceived severity (e.g., a "violent" attack) – and thus harm – also came into their participants' typical conceptions. In neither study did participants include assaults against women as part of their conception of a hate crime. In fact, in the scenarios used in Craig and Waldo's Study 2, when a woman was attacked and her race, religion or sexual orientation unspecified, the authors merely classified this as ambiguous.

Accordingly, in this research we aim to explore why gender does not fit into people's conceptions of a hate crime. According to Prototype Theory, it may be because gender-motivated hate crimes 1) do not fit the typical victim-perpetrator demographics, 2) are not perceived as carrying discriminatory intent, and/or 3) are not viewed as serious enough to meet standards of harm. Thus, to the extent that we can manipulate the presence or absence of variables that affect perceptions of intent or harm, we might see an increase in the perception that crimes targeting women may be bias-motivated and thus merit the label "hate crime." We will review each aspect in turn.

Victim-Perpetrator Demographics

Demographics can influence whether or not a situation is labeled as a hate crime. In particular, characteristics of the victim (e.g., minority status), characteristics of the perpetrator (e.g., majority status), and characteristics of the victim-perpetrator relationship (e.g., boss-employee in workplace scenarios, strangers in hate crime scenarios) all come into play. Although many gender-motivated hate crimes may fit the prototype with regard to perpetrator demographics - with the perpetrator being male as is typical of instances of civil sex discrimination – a crime targeting a woman does not fit the prototypical victim mold. Indeed, in the few studies that have examined hate crimes targeting women, people do not consider crimes against women to be hate crimes. For example, in Saucier and colleagues' (2006) study, participants responded to vignettes of court cases in which the type of assault (simple versus aggravated) and victim group membership varied. They found that a crime committed against a minority group was more likely to be considered a hate crime compared to crimes against women. The same crime targeting a minority (African-Americans, Asian-American, Latinos, Jews, or gay men) was thus more likely to also receive a heavier sentence than a crime targeting a woman.

Hertl and Sinclair (2008) also showed that gender-motivated crimes do not fit the conception of a typical hate crime. Across two studies, it was found that scenarios featuring a female victim of any race were significantly less likely to be labeled a hate crime than a scenario featuring an African American male. Additional factors influenced participants' perceptions. For example, if the scenario featured the combination of sexual assault and acquaintanceship this was unlikely to be labeled as a hate crime, but only when targeting a woman of any race and not when targeting a male African-American. Also, the presence of derogatory slurs increased the application of the hate crime label to gender-based crimes, but not so much that the crime was labeled a hate crime as frequently as when the victim was African-American. Accordingly, even when taking additional factors into account, victim demographics -- non-prototypical (women) vs. prototypical (African-American) – still explained the bulk of the variance in the application of the hate crime label.

An additional problem that arises with regard to "gendered" crime is that crimes targeting women are typically perpetrated by someone known to them (Koss, Goodman, Fitzgerald, Keita, & Russo, 1994). As such, the prototype of "violence against women" as intimate may conflict with the prototype of a hate crime which is perceived as perpetrated by strangers (Boyd et al., 1996; Weisburd & Levin, 1994). Indeed, as mentioned above in the description of the Hertl and Sinclair study, when acquaintanceship between the victim and perpetrator was manipulated it reduced the likelihood that the hate crime label was applied to gender crimes. This effect was not seen when the crime targeted an African-American. However, in that study, there was a limitation in the operationalization of victim-perpetrator relationship, because the acquaintance in the gender scenario was an ex-intimate while the acquaintance in the race scenario was a former co-worker. Accordingly, the present study will remedy this by keeping the level of intimacy equivalent.

Perceived Intention

In addition to demographics, perpetrator intention is another important element in the prototype model. Intent and motive are closely linked concepts and a hate crime is a crime defined by its motive. In order to determine whether a crime merits the label of hate or bias-motivated, one must gauge both the motive and intent of the perpetrator. In fact, Swim, Sechrist, Scott, Campbell, and Stangor (2003) found that perceived harm of a discriminatory incident does not have a significant effect on labeling when the perpetrator is assumed to have intentions to discriminate. Thus perceiving the intent to be biased appears an essential, if not over-riding, feature of labeling acts - violent and non-violent - of discrimination. Although some legal scholars argue that motive precedes intent - e.g., the motive being the drive behind the act and the intent addressing whether the individual meant to act on that motive - the prototype model put forth by Harris and colleagues seems to take a slightly different stance. Although their paper did not clearly differentiate between intent and motive, for the purposes of the present study we interpret the model as putting perceiving that the individual intended to discriminate when committing a particular action as a precursor to perceiving the act as discriminatory (and thus perceiving discriminatory motives). Thus, although when the actor is committing the action, motive might precede or go hand-in-hand with intent, when observers are judging a situation the perception of intent might precede the perception of motive. At least, the prototype model would suggest the need to see the perpetrator's actions towards the particular target as purposeful - as opposed to accidental or secondary to another intent - before perceiving the act as being driven by bias.

With regard to the issue of intent, acquaintanceship between the victim and perpetrator presents another problem aside from simply the acquaintance defying the conception of a typical stranger relationship. Victim-perpetrator demographics are also linked to perceived intention. Sorting intention may be a problem in gender-motivated crimes because it will be seen as something personal, private, and specific to the person, not political or driven by discrimination against any random member(s) of a group. Thus, the perpetrator may have intended to try to hurt the victim, but did not intend to discriminate against women in targeting this particular victim. In a study by Hertl and Sinclair (2008) it was shown that motives of "revenge," "retaliation for rejection," and "sexual" were far more likely to be applied to gender crimes than parallel incidents featuring an African-American male victim. In the case of the African-American victims, "hate/bias/prejudice" was the most common motive applied, even when robbery was included as a potential alternative explanation for the perpetrator behavior.

Building off this existing research, in the present study we will be purposefully manipulating possible interpretations of perpetrator intent by increasing the salience of the victim's group affiliation in the scenario. In the prototypical situation, the victim will be returning from a political meeting. The purpose of this manipulation is to see whether affiliating the victim with a group-specific political organization (e.g., NAACP or NOW) will result in a higher rate of application of the hate crime label. Having the victim targeted outside of the group's headquarters may make the intent of the perpetrator more evident by way of his selection of the victim. In fact, this was unintentionally manipulated by Hertl and Sinclair (2008) when they had victims in Study 1 coming from a political rally. Study 1 received higher rates of the application of the hate crime label than did Study 2 where the victims were coming from a study group. Further, it is anticipated that manipulating the victim-perpetrator relationship will also affect perceived perpetrator motives, leading participants to see the attack as more personal and thus less motivated by bias against a group.

Perceived Harm

A last factor we will be examining will be the level of perceived harm. Consistent with the Harris et al. (2004) model, Swim and colleagues (2003) identified perceived intention as a factor that will lead people to label a situation as an act of discrimination. However, intent was not the only factor examined. Swim et al. (2003) ran four experiments in which they examined how an actor's intent as well as the harm experienced by a target influenced judgments of prejudice and discrimination. They found that the greater the harm caused by the action, the more likely it was to be perceived as an act of discrimination particularly when intent was ambiguous.

Specific to hate crime research, Saucier et al. (2006) presented court case vignettes to participants to examine perceptions of hate crimes. In the vignettes, severity of crime (simple assault and aggravated assault) and group membership (race, gender, etc.) were manipulated. Consistent with the Prototype model and their hypotheses, they found that a more violent attack was more likely to be labeled a hate crime.

However, gender-based discrimination – violent or non-violent – may face a hurdle when it comes to perceptions of severity. For example, when Cowan and Hodge (1996) administered scenarios to participants describing incidents of hate speech, they found that ethnic speech was rated more offensive, and thus more harmful, by participants than either gender or gay targeted speech. As such, gender-based discrimination - be it in the workplace, hate speech, or hate crimes - might not meet the threshold of the level of perceived harm expected of acts of prototypical discrimination.

In fact, gender-motivated crimes may need to meet a higher threshold of criteria. According to Hertl and Sinclair (2008), gender-motivated crimes needed to include group derogatory slurs and be physical attacks - not sexual attacks - by explicitly specified strangers to even potentially merit the hate crime label. However, even with these criteria met, most gender-based attacks were still not identified as hate crimes with the same frequency as a scenario based upon race. It is important to note, though, that these incidents were still rated as quite serious, regardless of whether they targeted a woman or an African-American. Accordingly, perceived seriousness and harm may not be as important to identifying discrimination as the Prototype model asserts (see also Swim et al., 2003).

The Difficulty of Labeling Gender-Motivated Hate Crimes

So why might people have such difficulty applying the hate crime label to gender-based attacks? If we apply the Prototype model, it becomes clear that gender-based attacks do not fit. For example, simply by virtue of women being targeted, the crime is less likely to be labeled a hate crime because the prototypical hate crime targets someone based on race, religion, or sexual orientation (Craig & Waldo, 1996; Saucier et al., 2006). Further, gender-based attacks fail on victim-perpetrator demographics as well because the typical violence against women is perpetrated by an acquaintance, but the typical hate crime is perpetrated by a stranger (Weisburd & Levin, 1994). Also, the intent of the perpetrator in choosing a female victim might be blurred by other factors (e.g., victim-perpetrator relationship makes the selection of the victim seem less based on gender) thus gender-motivated attacks do not clearly meet the prejudiced intention criteria either. Lastly, there is some evidence that gender-based attacks may even fail on the third criteria of the prototype model, perceived harm/severity. According to some, attacks on women, especially those in the context of an acquaintanceship between victim and perpetrator, are minimized (Koss et al., 1994) and discrimination against women (e.g., hate speech) is not taken as seriously as other types of discrimination (Cowan & Hodge, 1996). All of these factors combine to make perceiving discrimination in gender-based attacks more difficult, and consequently labeling any potential gender-discriminatory violence as a "hate crime" less likely.

Of interest to the present study are the factors indicated by the prototype model, namely, victim (and victim-perpetrator) demographics, perceived intention, and perceived harm. Thus, the purpose of the present research is to manipulate these aforementioned variables to examine the impact on the perception of the discriminatory motive and, thus, the application of the hate crime label. To do this, we will take a scenario previously used by Hertl and Sinclair (2008) and manipulate Victim Type (Prototypical: *African-American* female [and race-specific slurs], Non-prototypical: White *female* [and gender-specific slurs]), Severity of Assault (Non-Prototypical: Simple Assault vs. Prototypical: Aggravated), Location (Group-relevant: Following a group-based political event [e.g., National Organization of Women or National Association for the Advancement of Colored People], Group-Irrelevant: Following a class), and Type of Victim-Perpetrator Relationship (Prototypical: Stranger, Non-prototypical: Intimate) to examine whether reductions or increases in perceived discriminatory motives and the application of the hate crime label occur. Victim type and victim-perpetrator relationship variables are included to tap the role of victim-perpetrator demographics. Severity of Assault is included to potentially manipulate perceived harm. Group-relevant versus group-irrelevant location is included to manipulate clarity of intent, as waiting outside a group organizational meeting for a potential victim implies more effort went into selecting a victim of a certain type. Note, however, that victim-perpetrator relationship could also serve to address both the issue of harm and intent to discriminate. Victim-perpetrator acquaintanceship blurs the line of intent/motive to discriminate because when the victim is acquainted with her perpetrator the attack may be perceived as a personal attack, not a political or group-based attack. Also, Weisburd and Levin (1994) suggest that stranger assaults are taken more seriously than crimes between individuals known to one another. Thus, crimes featuring acquainted persons may be viewed as less harmful.

The present study represents an extension of existing research by including the following variables already identified as important: Victim Type, Severity of Assault, and Victim-Perpetrator Relationship. However, this study is unique from preceding research as it not only combines these variables but also adds in Location, and includes a balanced manipulation of Victim Type (by keeping both victims female and just manipulating whether race or gender is salient) that allows for us to also have a clearer manipulation of intimacy of Victim-Perpetrator relationship (ex-partner or stranger).

We expect to find that:

H1 – Crimes targeting the non-prototypic victim – a white female - will be less likely to be perceived as discriminatory and labeled less often as a hate crime than the same crime targeting a more prototypic person – an African-American female.

H2 – The presence of additional counter-prototypic variables – such as acquaintanceship – will reduce the perception of discriminatory motives and the application of the hate crime label relative to the more prototypic stranger condition.

H3 – A crime targeting the victim outside of the group's political headquarters will increase the perception of bias motives and the application of the hate crime label.

H4 – A more violent attack may be more likely to be seen as discriminatory and will be more likely to be labeled as a hate crime, as more harmful crimes are more prototypical of a hate crime.

In conclusion, gender-motivated hate crimes are not generally perceived as being hate crimes. Gender does not fit the general prototype of a hate crime for the vast majority of people.

Through research (e.g., Hertl & Sinclair, 2008; Saucier et al., 2006) it has been found that there are certain factors that lead to an increase in the application of the bias crime label. Building off this research, we chose to add or modify different variables established as important previously. We expect to discover which variables carry the most weight when determining whether a particular crime warrants the label "hate crime."

METHOD

Participants

Participants were 252 students (111 men, 141 women) recruited from introductory psychology classes at a mid-size Southeastern university. 75.2% of the sample was Caucasian, 18.8% were African-American, and the remaining 6.0% were Asian-American, Hispanic, mixed race, or other. The mean age for this sample was 19.80 (SD = 2.05). Participants were awarded class credit for their participation.

Design

This study employed a 2 Victim Type (Prototypical: African-American female, Non-prototypical: White female), x 2 Severity of Assault (Prototypical: Aggravated Assault, Non-prototypical: Simple), x 2 Location (Prototypical: Group-Relevant/Political, Non-prototypical: Group-Irrelevant/Campus) x 2 Type of Victim-Perpetrator Relationship (Prototypical: Stranger, Non-prototypical: Intimate) between-subjects design.

Materials and Procedure

Participants were recruited to participate in a study titled "Classifying Crimes." The participants took the survey online through the Sona-systems research administration program. Once participants registered on the website, they were assigned a login that was a combination of their initials and a randomly generated 2-3 digit number. The number was used to randomly assign the subjects to conditions, such that depending on the randomly generated code, participants only saw the one survey open to. For example, participants whose IDs ended in 00-05 only saw the first condition.

Upon accessing the survey information, participants were instructed that they would receive a newspaper account of an incident. Before they read the scenario, participants were told in the consent form that if they avoid exposure to violent media, or are otherwise sensitive to offensive language, descriptions of victimization, and/or violent behavior they should not participate. The participants were also told that if they felt uncomfortable at any time to withdraw from the study by exiting their browser window. Eight participants in total withdrew from the study, all their information was automatically erased, and thus they are not included in the sample. For the remaining 252, the survey took an average of approximately twelve minutes to complete (SD = 4.74).

Stimulus Materials

In the first section of the survey, participants were given one scenario to read. The scenarios were based on a scenario used by Hertl and Sinclair (2008), which drew from the scenario used by Craig and Waldo (1996). The aspects that were changed across the scenarios were Victim Type, Severity of Assault, Location, and Victim-Perpetrator Demographics. The variables that were manipulated have been italicized in the following scenario.

> On March 15th, 2002 at 10:30 p.m., a *young white woman* was physically assaulted in the southeastern section of the Chicago suburb, Triton, after having been followed from her *college class*. The assailants were described as two white males in their early twenties. The first assailant jumped the victim from behind and the second assailant ran over from across the street and joined in the attack, *stabbing the victim*, and tearing her t-shirt. The assailants broke off the attack and fled when cars and a pedestrian stopped at the scene. The assailants were heard *yelling "whore," "bitch," and "cunt"* at the victim by the onlooker. They got away with, at least, the victim's backpack and ring. In keeping with typical protocol, police are checking for any activity on her stolen credit cards. The victim was quickly taken to a hospital where she is currently hospitalized. The victim was *able to identify* the *second assailant as an ex-boyfriend*.

Victim Type was manipulated by having half of the scenarios describe the victim as an African-American female, while the other half described the victim as a White female. Further, gender versus race was made salient by the use of gender or race (i.e., "nigger," "monkey," "tar baby") derogatory slurs. Location was manipulated by having half of the scenarios describe the victim as coming from a college class, while the other half had the victim coming from a National Organization for Women or a National Association for the Advancement of Colored People meeting. The type of meeting matched the victim type. Severity of Assault was manipulated by having half of the scenarios describe the victim being physically assaulted and the assault involved a weapon (e.g., "stabbed"), while in the other half the victim was assaulted physically but there was no weapon (no stabbing). Type of Victim-Perpetrator Relationship was manipulated by having the victim not being able to identify the assailants in half of the scenarios, while in the other half the victim identified one of the assailants as an ex-boyfriend.

Dependent Variable Materials

After participants read the scenario they completed some open-ended questions (e.g., "what headline would you apply," "what label do you think best fits the scenario") to ensure that they thought about and processed the scenario. Also, this format was chosen because it allowed the participants to freely apply the "hate crime" label in the open-ended section without being specifically prompted "do you think this was a hate crime?" The participants were also asked what they thought motivated the offenders.

Following the scenario and initial open-ended responses, the participant submitted the first section of the survey and proceeded to the second section window. Within these forced-choice questions, there were two primary dependent variables of interest. These were Perceived Bias Motive and the Application of the Hate Crime Label.

Perceived Bias Motive. To assess whether the participant perceived that the incident was motivated by prejudice, and thus, discriminatory, participants were asked to what extent they believed the motive of the perpetrator was religious/moral, prejudice/bias against victim, power, sexual, the perpetrator felt rejected, personal vendetta, hate, insanity, cause fear/terrorize/harass, terrorize the community, greed, thrill-seeking, intimacy-seeking, and other than what was listed. For each charge, the participant could respond on a 5-point Likert scale where $0 = Not\ at\ all$ and $4 = Extremely$. We provided an array of options so that the participant would not feel obliged to assess prejudice alone as a motive, but it was ultimately the perceived prejudice motive item that was the dependent variable of interest.

Hate Crime Label. To assess labeling, participants were similarly asked how likely they would be to label the scenario as a sexual assault, domestic violence, school violence, robbery, harassment/stalking, simple assault, aggravated assault, terroristic threats, murder, attempted murder, rape/sodomy, and hate crime. For each charge, the participant could respond on a 5-point Likert scale where $0 = Not\ at\ all$ and $4 = Extremely\ likely$. Thus, the hate crime option was just one of multiple charges the participant could choose as applicable. Again, we did this intentionally, so that participants would not feel obliged to simply weight the application of the "hate crime" label.

Manipulation Checks

Lastly, participants completed some personal information (e.g., demographics) as well as being administered manipulation checks. Open ended questions were used to verify that the participant recalled the race and gender of the victim and perpetrators as well as recalled the location of the crime and the nature of the victim-perpetrator relationship. Also, participants were asked three forced choice questions to assess perceptions of incident severity to ensure that Severity of Assault variable sufficiently affected perceptions of the incident. These questions included: how harmful they thought the incident was to the victim, how serious they thought the crime was, and how severely they thought the perpetrator should be punished (*0 = Not at all, 4 = Extremely*).

After completing the demographics and remaining manipulation checks, participants submitted their responses to this third section and then saw the debriefing screen. Participants were automatically awarded the appropriate credit for their participation.

RESULTS

The purpose of this study was to provide participants with a description of a crime wherein variables related to the Harris et al. (2004) Prototype model (e.g., victim demographics, level of harm) were manipulated. The manipulation of these aforementioned variables was done to examine their impact on the perception of prejudice as an underlying motive and, consequently, the application of the hate crime label. It was believed that: (1) Crimes targeting the non-prototypic victim – a white female - would be labeled less often as a hate crime than the same crime targeting a more prototypic person – an African-American female. (2) A crime targeting the victim outside of group-relevant location (e.g., race-relevant: NAACP; gender-relevant: NOW) would increase the application of the hate crime label than crimes outside a more generic location (e.g., a college campus). The group's location was intended to make group identity more salient and the intentionality of the perpetrator's selection of the victim more evident. (3) The presence of additional counter-prototypic variables, such as acquaintanceship, should also reduce the application of the hate crime label as compared to the same crime committed by the prototypic stranger. (4) Lastly, more violent attack was believed to potentially be more likely to be labeled as a hate crime, as more harmful crimes are more prototypical of hate crimes and prototype models of discrimination labeling have identified severity of incident as a contributing factor to identifying prejudice as a motive.

The extent to which participants believed the motive of the perpetrator was prejudice/bias against the victim was assessed by a forced choice question asking to what extent the participant felt the incident was motivated by "prejudice/bias" (0 = *not at all, 4 = definitely*). Applying the hate crime label was assessed by a forced choice question to determine if they would press "hate crime" charges (0 = *not at all, 4 = definitely*). Results were analyzed using hierarchical regressions. MANOVAs were also employed to explore any potential interactions of the independent variables, although no interactions were explicitly predicted in the hypotheses. The results of the hierarchical regressions will be addressed first. Results regarding the motive dependent variable will be followed by the findings for the labeling of the crime.

Manipulation Checks

Before proceeding to the results, it is important to verify that the participants viewed the more severe attack as more serious as well as to check that participants were able to accurately pick up on details about the crime (e.g., race, gender, location, relationship). For victim type, only two participants failed to accurately identify that the victims were female, all identified the perpetrator gender correctly. Two individuals failed to accurately identify the race of the perpetrator, and one failed to accurately identify the race of the victim. Another seven individuals failed to identify that the victim and perpetrator were acquainted in the acquaintance scenario (one of whom also misidentified the victim race). These mistakes did not occur in the stranger scenario. In the group-relevant location, eleven individuals incorrectly described the location, and twelve did so in the college campus condition (five of these individuals were those who made other mistakes elsewhere). All analyses were conducted with and without these 29 individuals and the results were not dramatically affected by their elimination, so we retained the original sample.

We also asked participants to make assessments of the severity of the crime described. We asked questions such as "how harmful do you think the incident was to the victim," "how serious do you think the incident was," and "how severely do you think the perpetrators should be punished?" These items were responded to on a 5-point Likert scale (*0 = not at all, 4 = extremely*), and were combined to form our "Severity Index" (α = .77). The Severity score was then used as a dependent variable in an ANOVA including all of the independent variables. Only one significant main effect emerged for Attack Severity [$F(1,235)$ = 9.17, p = .003, eta^2 = .04], such that the aggravated assault (M = 3.31, SD = 0.71) was rated as more serious than the simple assault (M = 3.02, SD = 0.66). Thus our manipulation of Attack Severity was successful.

Hypothesis Testing: Motive

Moving onto hypothesis testing, our first step was to examine which variables affected the dependent variable of motive a hierarchical regression was run. The motive model included two steps: Step 1 included the Participant's Gender (coded *0 = male, 1 = female*) and Participant's Race (*0 = white* and *1 = racial minority*). Step 2 added the Victim Type (*0 = White female, 1 = African American female*), Location [*0 = General (Campus), 1 = Group-Relevant*], Victim-Perpetrator Relationship (*0 = Stranger, 1 = Acquainted*), and Severity of Assault (*0 = Simple Assault, 1 = Aggravated Assault*). The Participant's Gender and Race were entered first as a means for controlling for them. Although we did not include participant demographics in our hypotheses, individual differences – such as observer demographics - are included in Harris et al.'s (2004) Prototype model as potentially relevant.

Overview of Results for Motive. The overall mean for the application of the bias motive was 2.25 (SD = 1.37). In Step 1 of the motive hierarchical regression, we found R^2 = .01, and the model was non-significant [$F(2, 244)$ = 0.39, p = NS]. Thus, the participant demographics did not predict the perception of the prejudice motive. However, in Step 2 there was a significant $\triangle R^2$ = .26, and the model became significant [$F(6,240)$ = 13.91, p < .0005]. A summary of hierarchical regression analysis for variables predicting the perception of bias motive can be found in Table 1.

Victim Type. Victim Type was a significant predictor of the extent to which participants perceived the perpetrator was motivated by prejudice or bias (b = 1.24, SE = 0.15, β = 0.45, p < .0005). Consistent with our hypothesis, the crimes targeting a white female (M = 1.59, SD = 1.33) – the non-prototypic victim - were less likely to be perceived as prejudice or bias as a motive than crimes targeting a more prototypic victim (i.e., an African American female, M = 2.87, SD = 1.11) even though both crimes could be seen as intergroup (i.e., white on black, male on female).

Table 1. Summary of Hierarchical Regression Analysis for Variables Predicting the Perception of Bias Motive (N = 252)

	STEP ONE			STEP TWO		
VARIABLE	B	SE	β	B	SE	β
Participant Gender	0.15	0.18	0.06	0.19	0.16	0.07
Participant Race	-0.01	0.21	-0.00	-0.01	0.18	-0.00
Victim Type				1.24	0.15	0.45***
Location				0.30	0.15	0.11*
Relationship				-0.42	0.15	-0.15**
Assault Severity				0.13	0.15	0.05

*$p < .05$, **$p < .01$, ***$p < .001$.

Note. $R^2 = .00$ for Step 1; $\triangle R^2 = .26$ for Step 2; [$F(2, 244) = 0.39$, $p = $ NS]for Step 1; [$F(6,240) = 13.91$, $p < .0005$]for Step 2. Participant's Gender (*0 = male, 1 = female*); Participant's Race (*0 = white, 1 = racial minority*); Victim Type (*0 = White female, 1 = African American female*); Location (*0 = General, 1 = Group Relevant*); Victim-Perpetrator Relationship (*0 = Stranger, 1 = Acquainted*); Severity of Assault (*0 = Simple Assault, 1 = Aggravated Assault*).

Location. We also examined whether a crime targeting the victim outside of a group-relevant location would increase the extent to which prejudice was perceived as the likely motive. Location was found to be influential for the extent to which the participant saw bias as motivating perpetrator actions ($b = 0.30$, $SE = 0.15$, $\beta = 0.11$, $p = .05$). Consistent with our hypothesis, if the incident took place outside a group-relevant location ($M = 2.43$, $SD = 1.38$), instead of a generic location ($M = 2.10$, $SD = 1.36$), the extent to which prejudice was perceived as the motive increased.

Type of Victim-Perpetrator Relationship. In our third hypothesis, we expected to find that the victim and perpetrator being acquainted with each other, as opposed to strangers, would reduce the extent to which participants perceived prejudice as the motive. The regression revealed a significant effect for Type of Victim-Perpetrator Relationship on the extent to which prejudice was perceived as the motive ($b = -0.42$, $SE = 0.15$, $\beta = -0.15$, $p = .007$) such that acquaintanceship between the victim and perpetrator ($M = 2.00$, $SD = 1.34$) did reduce the perception of prejudicial motives (Stranger: $M = 2.52$, $SD = 1.36$).

Severity of Assault. The last thing we examined was whether more violent attacks would be more likely to be perceived as motivated by prejudice against the victim. Contrary to the hypothesis, and thus contrary to the prototype model, attack severity was not found to have a significant effect on the extent to which prejudice or bias was seen as the motive in the scenario ($b = 0.12$, $SE = 0.15$, $\beta = 0.05$, $p = $ NS, Aggravated: $M = 2.31$, $SD = 1.35$; Simple: $M = 2.19$, $SD = 1.40$).

Hypothesis Testing: Hate Crime Label

The application of the hate crime label regression model included three steps. The first two steps mirrored those of the analysis for motive. Step 1 included Participant's Race and Participant's Gender. Step 2 added Victim Type, Location Type, Victim-Perpetrator Relationship, and Severity of Assault. Lastly, in Step 3 the previous DV of whether participants felt prejudice was the underlying motive was entered as an additional predictor. After all, hate crimes are defined by the motive – i.e., also called bias-*motivated* crimes – and thus it seems important to assess the extent to which the perceived motive accounts for the application of the label. It could be that the impact of the independent variables on the dependent variable is completely mediated by perceived motive.

Table 2. Summary of Hierarchical Regression Analysis for Variables Predicting Application of the Hate Crime Label (N = 252)

VARIABLE	STEP ONE			STEP TWO			STEP THREE		
	B	SE	β	B	SE	β	B	SE	β
Participant Gender	0.22	0.18	0.08	0.27	0.16	0.09[+]	0.16	0.13	0.05
Participant Race	0.14	0.21	0.04	0.12	0.18	0.04	0.12	0.15	0.04
Victim Type				1.38	0.15	0.49***	0.68	0.14	0.24***
Location				0.34	0.15	0.12*	0.17	0.13	0.06
Relationship				-0.31	0.15	-0.11*	-0.07	0.13	-0.02
Assault Severity				0.32	0.15	0.12*	0.25	0.13	0.09*
Prejudice Motive							0.57	0.05	0.56***

$+p < .09$ $*p < .05$, $***p < .001$.

Note. $R^2 = .00$ for Step 1; $\triangle R^2 = .26$ for Step 2; $[F(2,244) = 1.06$, $p = $ NS, $R^2 = .01]$ for Step 1; $[F(6,240) = 17.17$, $p < .0005$, $R^2 = .30]$ for Step 2; $[F(7,239) = 38.42$, $p < .0005$, $R^2 = .53]$ for Step 3. Participant's Gender ($0 = male$, $1 = female$); Participant's Race ($0 = white$, $1 = racial minority$); Victim Type ($0 = White female$, $1 = African American female$); Location ($0 = General$, $1 = Group Relevant$); Victim-Perpetrator Relationship ($0 = Stranger$, $1 = Acquainted$); Severity of Assault ($0 = Simple Assault$, $1 = Aggravated Assault$).

Overview of Results for Hate Crime Label. The overall mean for the application of the hate crime label was 2.40 (SD = 1.41). In Step 1 of the application of the hate crime label model was non-significant [$F(2,244)$ = 1.06, p = NS, R^2 = .01]. Thus, participant demographics alone did not contribute anything to either of the models. However, once the independent variables were entered in Step 2 there was a significant $\triangle R^2$ = .29 and the model became significant [$F(6,240)$ = 17.17, p < .0005, R^2 = .30]. Including the perceived motive in Step 3 further added to the model. There was a significant $\triangle R^2$ = .23 yielding a significant final model [$F(7,239)$ = 38.42, p < .0005, R^2 = .53]. We will now discuss each result in turn as relevant to hypotheses. A summary of hierarchical regression analysis for variables predicting the application of the hate crime label can be found in Table 2.

Victim Type. It was expected that crimes targeting a non-prototypic victim would be labeled less often as a hate crime than the same crime targeting a more prototypic person. Consistent with hypotheses, Victim Type was a significant predictor of the application of the Hate Crime label to the scenario at both Steps (Step 2: b = 1.38, SE = 0.15, β = 0.49, p < .0005; Step 3: b = 0.68, SE = 0.14, β = 0.24, p < .0005). The crimes targeting a white female (M = 1.67, SD = 1.33) were less likely to be labeled a hate crime than crimes targeting an African American female (M = 3.08, SD = 1.11). This effect remained even after perceived motive was accounted for in Step 3.

Location. A second hypothesis examined whether a crime targeting the victim outside of a group-relevant location would increase the application of the hate crime label (potentially due to making the intergroup nature of the crime more salient). Location was significant in Step 2 (b = 0.34, SE = 0.15, β = 0.12, p = .028), but it was not found to be significant for the application of the hate crime label in Step 3 (b = 0.17, SE = 0.13, β = 0.06, p = NS, Group-relevant Location: M = 2.59, SD = 1.42; Generic Location: M = 2.24, SD = 1.39). Once motive was included in the regression model for predicting hate crime labeling Location became non-significant. This suggests that motive perception might mediate the relationship between Location and the labeling of the hate crime. To test this potential mediating effect, a Sobel test was run using both an Interactive Calculation Tool for Mediation Tests (Preacher & Leonardelli, 2003) and Stata. The Location mediation test was marginally significant (Sobel t = 1.86, p = .06). Stata revealed that the mediation effect of the Prejudice Motive accounted for 65% of the total effect of Location on the application of the Hate Crime Label. A summary of the Sobel results can be found in Figure 2.

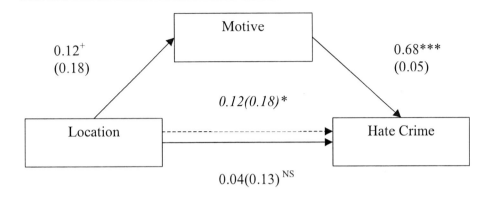

Sobel = 1.85, p = .063

+p<.06, *p<.05, ***p<.001
Note: Dashed line represents unmediated effect values.
Beta values and standard errors reported.

Figure 2. Results of Sobel Test Showing Mediation of the Relationship between Location and Hate Crime Labeling by Motive

Type of Victim-Perpetrator Relationship. A third hypothesis was that that the victim and perpetrator being acquainted with each other would reduce the application of the hate crime label. Type of Victim-Perpetrator Relationship had a marginal relationship to the application of the hate crime label in Step 2 (b = -0.31, SE = 0.15, β = -0.11, p = .05). However, it became non-significant in Step 3 (b = -0.07, SE = 0.13, β = -0.02, p = .61, Acquaintance: M = 2.20, SD = 1.38; Stranger: M = 2.60, SD = 1.43). Once motive was included in the regression model for predicting hate crime labeling Relationship became non-significant. A Sobel test was performed to test whether the relationship between Victim-Perpetrator Relationship and Hate Crime Labeling was mediated by Perceived Motive. The result of the Sobel test was highly significant (Sobel t = -2.96, p = .003). The mediation effect of the Extent of Prejudice accounted for 92% of the total effect of Relationship on the application of the Hate Crime Label. A summary of the Sobel results can be found in Figure 3.

Severity of Assault. The final hypothesis examined whether more violent attacks would be more likely to be labeled as a hate crime. Attack severity was found to be related for the application of the hate crime label to the scenario in both Steps (Step 2: b = 0.32, SE = 0.15, β = 0.12, p = .04); Step 3: b = 0.25, SE = 0.13, β = 0.09, p = .05). Consistent with the hypothesis, attack severity was found to have a significant effect on the extent to people perceived the act as a hate crime such that the aggravated assault (M = 2.55, SD = 1.36) was more likely to be labeled a hate crime than a simple assault (M = 2.24, SD = 1.46). This may be linked to hate crimes, generally, being regarded as more serious than non-hate motivated crimes – and, in fact, are often more harmful, degrading, and violent than the same crimes not motivated by prejudice (Boeckmann & Turpin-Petrosino, 2002; Iganski, 2001) – and thus, more severe attacks fit the prototype better even without affecting the perception of motive. In fact, application of the hate crime label was significantly positively correlated (r = 0.26) with the Severity Index (mentioned in the manipulation checks).

Exploring Potential Interactions between Independent Variables

Although no interactions were explicitly predicted in the hypotheses, to explore potential interactions a multivariate analysis of variance (MANOVA) was run with the Victim Type, Severity of Assault, Location, and Victim-Perpetrator Relationship as the independent variables and the Prejudice Motive and Hate Crime Label indices as the dependent variables (the DVs were correlated at r = 0.69). In the multivariate results, main effects were found for both Victim Type [Wilks Lambda (2,232) = 42.65, p = .0005, eta^2 = .27] and Location [Wilks Lambda (2,232) = 3.18, p = .04, eta^2 = .03]. A marginal main effect was found for Relationship [Wilks Lambda (2,232) = 2.78, p = .06, eta^2 = .02], while no significant main effect was found for Severity of Assault [Wilks Lambda (2,232) = 1.83, p = NS]. Also, no significant interactions were found at the multivariate level.

Examining the results at the univariate level, Victim Type was found to have a significant effect on both extent of prejudice [F(1,232) = 58.22, p = .0005, eta^2 = .20] and application of the hate crime label [F(1,232) = 75.31, p = .0005, eta^2 = .24]. Severity of Assault was found to have a marginal effect on the application of the hate crime label [F(1,232) = 3.49, p = .063 eta^2 = .02]. Location was found to have a significant effect on both the perception of motive [F(1,232) = 5.08, p = .025, eta^2 = .02] and application of the hate crime label [F(1,232) = 4.98, p = .027, eta^2 = .02]. Relationship was found to have a significant effect on the extent to which the participant believed bias was a motive for the perpetrator's actions [F(1,232) = 5.43, p = .021, eta^2 = .02]. All of these results, including the direction of the relationships (previously discussed), are largely consistent with the results of the hierarchical regressions.

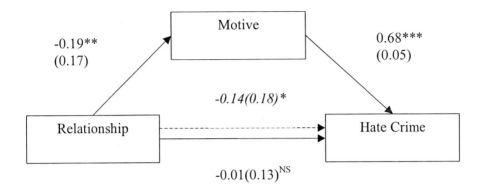

Sobel = -2.96, p = .003

*p<.05, **p<.01, ***p<.001
Note: Dashed line represents unmediated effect values
Beta values and standard errors reported.

Figure 3. Results of Sobel Test Showing Mediation of the Relationship between Victim-Perpetrator Relationship and Hate Crime Labeling by Motive

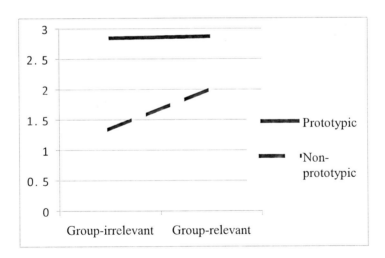

Figure 4. Significant Interaction Between Victim Type and Location on Motive

Aside from the main effects, only the interaction of Victim Type x Location for the Prejudice/Bias motive DV was found to be significant [$F(1,232) = 4.38$, $p = .037$, eta$^2 = .02$]. Overall, scenarios featuring an African American victim were more likely to be labeled a hate crime than those featuring a non-prototypic victim. However, if the attack on the non-prototypic victim took place in a group-relevant location, it increased the likelihood that individuals perceived a hate crime as having occurred than if the same victim was targeted on a college campus. The participants readily perceived the crime against the African-American victim as a hate crime, and location did little to change this perception. Victim demographics alone were sufficient when the victim fit the prototype. A summary of the interaction of Victim type x Location can be found in Figure 4.

DISCUSSION

The aim of the present study was to apply the prototype model to understand the factors that might contribute to individuals seeing the discrimination underlying potential instances of discriminatory violence. It was expected that the participants would be less likely to apply the hate crime label or see bias as a motive in certain scenarios. In particular, the scenarios that featured a non-prototypic victim, a group-irrelevant location, acquaintanceship between the victim and perpetrator, or a less violent attack were anticipated to be less likely to be seen as hate-motivated, and thus, less likely to be labeled a hate crime. Each of the hypotheses were largely confirmed with the exception of attack severity only affecting the extent to which participants applied the hate crime label but not affecting whether they saw bias as a motive in the situation. Overall, the majority of participants did apply the hate crime label if the scenario featured an African American victim, a group-relevant location, the victim and perpetrator were strangers, or the attack was more violent. These findings will be reviewed. However, before going further into the implications of the study, we will go over the caveats that should be considered as they might limit what conclusions can be drawn.

Caveats

It is important to note that one of the limitations of the study is that it was conducted with convenience samples. As we did not conduct the study with legal decision-makers or mock jurors, we are not able to necessarily generalize the findings to understanding why gender is rarely included in hate crime statutes or why, if it is included, it is rarely enforced. However, difficulty with the identification of gender-based hate crimes has previously been found in both samples of police officers (Boyd, et al., 1996) and lawyers (McPhail & DiNitto, 2005). Thus, some evidence exists that the problems exhibited by our convenience sample exist in the legal realm as well. Conducting the present study allowed us to focus in on which factors may in fact be causing some of the confusion found among officials in other studies. Accordingly, even with these limitations the current study still had results that were consistent with previous research on bias crimes. Indeed, the present study indicates factors that may affect perceptions of hate crimes overall – not just solely gender-motivated crimes – as there were few interactions. All of the main effects indicate that certain factors (e.g., victim-perpetrator relationship, level of harm) can affect cross-race crimes as well as crimes that are just cross-gender and not cross-race.

However, this study is limited by the fact that all the scenarios depicted female victims. We may not have found interactions because the victims were all female. There may be some factors that do uniquely affect gender-based crimes, but because both of our scenarios featured cross-gender crimes, we may not be able to see it. Keeping the gender equivalent across scenarios was necessary to keep the perpetrator demographics the same across conditions as well as the keep the type of victim-perpetrator relationship used in the present study equivalent (e.g., an ex-intimate). We could not have an African-American male attacked by a white male who was an ex-boyfriend as then we would have been introducing sexual orientation as an additional factor. Future studies could use both male and female victims and use a less intimate acquaintanceship (e.g., neighbor, co-worker) or could also introduce the factor of sexual orientation as it seems likely that the perception of motive in a cross-race attack by an ex-boyfriend or ex-girlfriend within a gay relationship would also be affected by the intimacy between the actor and target.

The use of all female victims was also a limitation because not all gender-based bias crimes target women. Although the lack of male victims in the scenario is a limitation to the study, it should be noted that the majority of gender-based bias crimes still target women. However, future studies could introduce manipulations of both victim and perpetrator gender to see if gender-based crimes targeting men are also less likely to be labeled as hate crimes.

Review of Findings

With the caveats in mind, we turn to the findings and potential implications. As an overview of the results, we have created a slightly altered prototype model (see Figure 5) based on the results of the present study. This revised model is intended to be illustrative as opposed to a recommended revision. Obviously, more research is needed to establish whether actual adjustments to the model are needed. Indeed, the present research focused on situational variables that contribute to the perception of discrimination and the labeling of bias crimes, and did not really examine any individual difference variables. Thus, the role of individual differences remains to be explored further. However, as illustrated in the model, we draw direct lines to "consequences" – namely calling the incident a hate crime (and thus likely perceiving the crime a warranting a heavier sentence) – when our analyses indicated that a particular variable, such as victim type and attack severity, appeared to have a direct effect on labeling that was not wholly mediated by perceiving the act as motivated by prejudice. For other variables, such as victim-perpetrator relationship (a type of actor/target variable) and location (which we saw as potentially a type of intent variable), our results indicate that their primary effects are on whether the perpetrator's motives were perceived as biased, and that led to increases in applying the bias crime label. We will review the findings for each variable in turn.

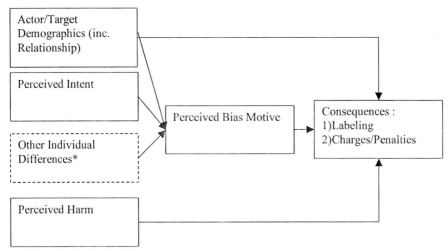

* Individual differences were used in the original Harris and colleagues (2004) Prototype Model. However, we found no significant effects for Participant Demographics, but perhaps other individual difference variables (e.g., sexism) would come into play.

Figure 5. New Conceptualization of the Harris and colleagues' (2004) Prototype Model

Victim Type

The first hypothesis dealt with victim type. It was hypothesized that people would be less likely to apply the hate crime label or recognize bias as a motive in a scenario featuring a non-prototypic victim (e.g., a white female) than a scenario featuring a more prototypic person (e.g., an African-American). Consistent with our hypotheses, victim demographics were the dominant independent variable affecting participants' perceptions of the motive and the label of the crime. The impact of victim demographics found in the present study was consistent with Saucier and colleagues' (2006) who also found that a crime committed against a minority group was more likely to be considered a hate crime than crimes against non-minority women. We found that not only does victim type independently affect the application of the label (i.e., the effect of victim type on hate crime labeling was not completely mediated by perceived motive), but it also affects the perception of the motive. Gender-only attacks were not perceived as motivated by prejudice.

It is interesting that this discrepancy in how individuals label motives and crimes exists simply based on victim type because the scenarios featuring the crime against the white woman carried the same elements as the crime against the minority woman in that it was the same type of attack, perpetrated by attackers of another demographic (i.e., men), and involved group-derogatory slurs. Note, we would expect the same finding were the attack on an African-American woman perpetrated by an African-American man. Thus, our finding seems to indicate that cross-racial crime is more readily identifiable as potentially bias-motivated than cross-gender crime. Other variables may enhance the likelihood that a cross-gender crime will be perceived as bias-motivated, but a gender-based attack seems to face a significant hurdle in being viewed as such due to the victim's demographic.

The potential impact of the prototype of a hate crime in the real world can be seen with regard to a recent shooting in Bridgeville, Pennsylvania. George Sodini opened fire in a women's aerobics class, killing three women and injuring nine (Rubinkam, 2009). Even though Sodini is described as hating women, the term "hate crime" has still not been widely applied to the shooting (Wade, 2009). Thus, although people, to some extent, see that Sodini "had a lot of hatred in him" (Candiotti, 2009), this "hate" does not seem to equate to perceiving the incident as a bias-motivated crime. Perhaps either because hatred of women is not seen as prejudice[1] or just that attacks on women even by someone who hates women do not fit the prototype of a "hate" crime. Sodini's crime causes one to ask whether this scenario would cause people to have the same debate about labeling had he opened fire and targeted only racial or religious minorities.

Location

To some extent, the application of the hate crime label to the potentially gender (as opposed to race) motivated attack was increased when the participant may have been reminded that the crime was still intergroup. Specifically, we examined how group-relevant and group-irrelevant locations affected the hate crime labeling and recognition of prejudice as a motive in the situation. We found that if the victim was assaulted outside of a group-relevant location, such as the NOW headquarters, the participants were more likely to perceive prejudice as a motive, and, in turn, label the incident a hate crime. However, this increase in the perception of prejudicial motives was really only seen for the crime targeting a white female. A crime against an African-American woman by a white male was already fairly readily seen as discriminatory, so there was little room for the addition of the NAACP headquarters to increase the perception that the perpetrators were motivated by prejudice. These results were consistent with the study by Hertl and Sinclair (2008) where they found that victims coming from a feminist political rally received a higher rate of application of the hate crime label than in other experiments where the scenarios did not feature the rally location.

Group-relevant location could potentially be useful in increasing the perception of bias motives for a number of reasons. Consistent with the Prototype model, location could make the intention of the perpetrator in selecting his victims more obvious (e.g., he went to the Holocaust Museum because he knew he'd have a better chance of finding a certain type of victim) and the attack less random.

---

[1] In follow-up analyses, a repeated-measures ANOVA was run with Victim Type as the between-subjects variable and Motive Type (Hate or Prejudice) as the within-subjects variable. And although there was a main effect of Victim Type [$F(1.247) = 29.76$, $p<.0005$], such that the attack against the prototypic victim ($M = 2.89$, $SD = 1.11$) was more likely to be seen as motivated by both hate and prejudice than the attack on the non-prototypic victim ($M = 1.98$, $SD = 1.37$), there was also a significant interaction of Victim Type and Motive Type. Attacks that were solely cross-gender were seen as hate-motivated ($M = 2.36$, $SD = 1.22$) more so than bias-motivated ($M = 1.59$, $SD = 1.33$). This difference in ascribing motives did not exist for the cross-race attacks (Hate: $M = 2.92$, $SD = 1.07$; Prejudice: $M = 2.87$, $SD = 1.11$). Thus, some evidence suggests to indicate that perceiving hate motivation does not equate to see prejudice motivation when the crime is cross-gender.

Location could also serve to increase the intergroup salience of the crime, by reminding the observer of the group membership of the victim and perpetrator. Also, political locations, in particular, may make the act seem more politically-motivated – and thus more consistent with a prototype of a hate crime – than personal. When these political locations are also of groups that strive for equality, participants may also be reminded of group inequalities that underlie discriminatory acts. Any of these could be reasons why location mattered for perceiving discriminatory motives. Future research could try to parse which of these – if not all of them – are the underlying reason for the impact of location on motive perceptions.

Future studies could vary a number of aspects about the location of the crime. For example, a manipulation could involve having the crime take place at a prototypical (e.g., a Jewish temple) vs. a less prototypical hate crime site (e.g., a personal residence) or vary the group-specific (e.g., a women-only reading group) vs. general location (e.g., book store). Also, manipulating whether that group-specific location was political and equal rights related or not could also help to determine the impact of the political aspect of the location. To determine why location matters, follow-up questions could then inquire how intentional the perpetrators acts were perceived to be, and gauge whether the intergroup nature of the crime was made more salient by asking questions like, "Were the perpetrator and victim of different demographic groups?"

Again, in the Sodini case, the perpetrator did go to a group-relevant location, namely a women's aerobics class. This location choice may have led to an increase in, at least, discussion of whether this crime was a hate crime as opposed to if the crime had occurred in a more generic location (e.g., like a school as in the attacks primarily or exclusively targeting girls in Jonesboro, Arkansas, Nickel, Pennsylvania, and Bailey, Colorado). However, given there is still debate about the application of the hate crime label to this incident, perhaps if the location had been both group-specific and political the relevance of the label would have been clearer. Future studies could explore whether a gender-motivated hate crime might need to occur at a political location as opposed to one where just women attend in order to increase the perception of bias motivation. This political standard regarding location may be unique to gender-based crimes, as other non-political but still group-relevant sites – like a gay bar - arguably still fit the prototype.

Relationship

Having an intimate relationship with one's attacker, however, seems not to fit the prototype. The relationship between the victim and the perpetrator in the crime was another element that affected the application of the perception of bias as a motive, and, thus, affected the application of the hate crime label. Victim-perpetrator relationship was examined because some have argued that acquaintanceship may be a unique hurdle facing gender-motivated crimes because the majority of violence against women is committed by someone familiar to the victim (e.g., Weisburd & Levin, 1994). The prototype is that hate crimes are committed by strangers (and, indeed, hate crimes targeting other groups are typically perpetrated by strangers, Weisburd & Levin, 1994). Accordingly, we investigated whether or not acquaintanceship reduced either the application of the hate crime label or the extent to which bias was perceived as a motive. Acquaintanceship mainly affected perceived motive. It did not directly affect labeling. Acquaintanceship reduced the extent to which prejudice was perceived as the motive and thus reduced the application of the hate crime label. Our results lend support to Weisburd and Levin's (1994) argument that people may have difficulty identifying gender-motivated hate crimes as motivated by bias because in most cases of violence against women – which are not necessarily hate-motivated – the victim and perpetrator are acquainted. Thus, there is a conflict between the prototype of "hate crime" and "violence against women." McPhail and DiNitto (2005) found that prosecutors in their study felt that violence against women, particularly that perpetrated by intimates, was motivated by love, power, and/or control, so the violence against women prototype may interfere with perceptions of motive[2].

However, potentially contrary to Weisburd and Levin's argument that acquaintanceship may uniquely affect perceptions of gender-motivated crime and wouldn't affect perceptions of hate crimes targeting more prototypic groups, we have some evidence that a relationship between the victim and perpetrator might

---

[2] Again, in follow-up analyses we did find that relationship affected whether the motives of personal vendetta, retaliation for rejection, or intimacy-seeking were ascribed to the perpetrator's actions. These more personal motives were assigned more in the intimate scenario than in the stranger condition (especially when the incident was only cross-gender). However, we did not get a significant difference in the extent to which "power and control" was assigned as a motive. This is interesting because although both scenarios were seen as involving elements of power and control as motives, this same motive means different things in one context versus another. Part of a hate crime is to exert one's dominance over another group (e.g., display power) and control out-groups (e.g., by punishing an African-American family for moving into a white neighborhood). However, exerting one's power and control over an intimate is not seen as being linked to bias.

prevent the application of the hate crime label even in situations featuring prototypic groups. After all, we did not find a significant interaction between victim type and victim-perpetrator relationship. Thus, the victim-perpetrator relationship did not uniquely affect the perception of the crime when it was only cross-gender and not cross-race. This lack of interaction may not be surprising, though, as both of the victims in the present study's scenarios were female. Thus, it could be that acquaintanceship may always affect the perception of the crime when the victim is female, even when that female victim fits a prototypic group as well. Also, as mentioned in the caveats, an intimate relationship, in particular, may universally affect the perception of whether a crime could be bias-motivated. After all, one might assume that if an individual was, at one point, in an intimate relationship with a person then s/he could not be biased against that individual. Future research could examine whether or not acquaintanceship affects cross-racial crimes that are not also cross-gender. Degrees of acquaintanceship are also worth investigating.

We must qualify our discussion that a null finding (i.e., the lack of an interaction between Victim Type and Relationship) doesn't mean no finding exists, just that we didn't find it in the present research. Hertl and Sinclair (2008) found that when acquaintanceship between the victim and perpetrator was manipulated it reduced the likelihood that the hate crime label was applied to gender crimes. This effect was not seen when the crime targeted an African-American male. However, in that study, there was a limitation in the operationalization of victim-perpetrator relationship, because the acquaintance in the gender scenario was an ex-intimate while the acquaintance in the race scenario was a former co-worker. Accordingly, while some evidence exists to indicate that victim-perpetrator relationship may only affect perceptions of crimes against women, more research is needed.

Harm & Severity

The final variable we investigated was whether or not a more severe attack would cause an increase in the application of the hate crime label and perception of prejudice as a motive. The scenarios featuring the more severe attack were more likely to merit the application of the hate crime label, but attack severity did not affect the perception of prejudice as a motive. The application of the hate crime label results were consistent with Saucier et al. (2006) who found that a more violent attack was more likely to be labeled a hate crime. However, that we failed to find that the severity of the act affected the perception of discriminatory motives is contrary to the Harris et al. (2004) Prototype model that would suggest the greater the perceived harm of the discriminatory act, the more likely the observer is to see the act as discriminatory.

It is important to note that these results regarding incident harm are not entirely inconsistent with past research. Level of perceived harm has not been strongly connected to the Prototype model in other studies. Perceived seriousness and harm may not be as important to identifying discrimination as the Prototype model asserts (Hertl and Sinclair, 2008; Swim et al., 2003). It may be that, as Swim et al (2003) found when other factors are present that contribute more to people's perceptions of discriminatory motives – such as victim demographics and intent – that incident severity doesn't contribute as much to one's perception of prejudicial motives. On the other hand, we must again be cautious about interpreting the lack of a significant relationship. The null finding may be due to our manipulation or due to the fact that the Harris et al.'s (2004) model dealt with civil discrimination, whereas hate crimes are the most extreme form of discrimination and thus may already meet some sort of threshold of severity. Accordingly, the model may not have extended to discriminatory violence in the same way as it applies to less extreme types of discrimination.

At the same time, it is important to note that although our findings regarding the severity of the act indicate that perceived harm does not necessarily affect the extent to which individuals perceive the act as discriminatory, act severity does lead individuals to apply a more serious label – i.e., hate-motivated crime in addition to labeling the act aggravated assault – perhaps recognizing that it should carry a heavier sentence. The application of the hate crime label to the more severe attack may reflect that a more serious crime fits the hate crime prototype better, regardless of the perception of the perpetrator's motive. Boeckmann and Turpin-Petrosino (2002) and Iganski (2001) found that when comparing hate and non-hate motivated crimes, that the hate motivated crimes were more serious (e.g., degrading, resulting in more injury) than the same crime (e.g., an assault) that did not have prejudice as a motive. Thus, the prototypical hate crime is one that is more serious than a non-hate motivated crime.

In sum, the present study shows that gender-based bias crimes do not fit the prototype of a hate crime, and thus, this may explain why gender-motivated hate crimes have rarely been prosecuted (if gender is even included in hate crime legislation). With the recent passage of the Matthew Shepard Hate Crime Sentencing Enhancement act, "gender" is now included – along with sexual orientation, disability, and gender identity – in federal anti-hate crime laws. However, the inclusion of gender in the policies does not equate to enforcement (see McPhail & DiNitto, 2005). If individuals do not *see* how a crime against a woman might be bias-motivated then there would be no need to pursue the charge. Accordingly, in both research and the real world, we need to examine how to make what appears to be an invisible crime (Angel, 1999; McPhail, 2002), namely gender-motivated bias crimes, visible.

REFERENCES

Angel, M. (1999). Abusive boys kill girls just like abusive men kill women: Explaining the obvious. *Temple Political & Civil Rights Law Review, 8*, 283-309.

Boeckmann, R. & Turpin-Petrosino, C. (2002). Understanding the harm of hate crime. *Journal of Social Issues, 58*(2), 207-225.

Boyd, E. A., Berk, R. A. & Hammer, K. M. (1996). Motivated by hatred or prejudice: Categorization of hate-motivated crimes in two police divisions. *Law & Society Review, 30*, 819-849

Came, B., Burke, D., Ferzoco, G., O'Farreli, B. & Wallace, B. (1989). Montreal massacre: Railing against feminists, *Maclean's Magazine*, 12-18. Retrieved September 7, 2008, from LEXIS-NEXIS Academic database.

Candiotti, S. (August 5, 2009). Gym shooter 'had a lot of hatred' for women, society. Retrieved on August 27, 2009 from http://www.cnn.com/2009/ CRIME/08/05/pennsylvania.gym.shooting/

Cowan, G. & Hodge, C. (1996). Judgments of hate speech: The effects of target group, publicness, and behavioral responses of the target. *Journal of Applied Social Psychology, 26*, 355-374.

Craig, K. & Waldo, C. (1996). "So, what's a hate crime anyway?" Young adults' perceptions of hate crimes, victims, and perpetrators. *Law and Human Behavior, 20*, 113-129.

Harris, M., Lievens, F. & van Hoye, G. (2004). "I think they discriminated against me:" Using prototype theory and organizational justice theory for understanding perceived discrimination in selection and promotion situations. *International Journal of Selection & Assessment, 12*, 54-65.

Hertl, J. & Sinclair, H. C. (2008, June). *Application of prototype theory to perceptions of gender-motivated bias crimes*. Poster presented at the annual meeting of the Society for the Psychological Study of Social Issues, Chicago, IL.

Iganski, P. (2001). Hate crimes hurt more. *American Behavioral Scientist, 45*, 626-638.

Inman, M. & Baron, R. (1996). Influence of prototypes on perceptions of prejudice. *Journal of Personality & Social Psychology*, *70*, 727-739.

Koss, M. P., Goodman, L. A., Fitzgerald, L. F., Keita, G. P. & Russo, N. F. (1994). *No Safe Haven*. Washington, D.C.: APA books.

McPhail, B. (2002). Gender-bias hate crimes: A review. *Trauma, Violence, & Abuse*, *3*, 125-143.

McPhail, B. & DiNitto, D. (2005). Prosecutorial perspectives on gender-bias hate crimes. *Violence Against Women*, *11*, 1162-1185.

Preacher, K. J. & Leonardelli, G. J. (2003). Calculation for the Sobel Test. http://people.ku.edu/~preacher/sobel/sobel.htm

Rubinkam, M. (2009). Pa. gunman who killed 3 was bitter, lonely; Diary mined after shooting at fitness club. *The Boston Globe*, *2*. Retrieved August 6, 2009, from LEXIS-NEXIS Academic database.

Saucier, D., Brown, T., Mitchell, R. & Cawman, A. (2006). Effects of victims' characteristics on attitudes toward hate crimes. *Journal of Interpersonal Violence*, *21*, 890-909.

Swim, J., Sechrist, G., Scott, E., Campbell, B. & Stangor, C. (2003). The role of intent and harm in judgments of prejudice and discrimination. *Journal of Personality & Social Psychology*, *84*, 944-959.

United States Congress (101st Congress). (1990). *Hate Crime Statistics Act* (Public Law 101-275). Washington, DC.

Wade, L. (August 14, 2009) News coverage of the George Sodini Murder/Suicide. Retrieved August 27, 2009 from: http://contexts.org/socimages/2009/08/14/guest-post-dead-girls/

Weisburd, S. W. & Levin, B. (1994). "On the Basis of Sex": Recognizing gender-based bias crimes. *Stanford Law & Policy Review*, 21-47.

In: Psychology of Hate
Editors: Carol T. Lockhardt, pp.35-57

ISBN: 978-1-61668-050-3
© 2010 Nova Science Publishers, Inc.

Chapter 2

TOWARD A PSYCHOLOGICAL CONSTRUCT OF ENMITY

Christopher R. Jones[*,1] *and Chris Loersch*[2]

[1]The Ohio State University, Columbus, OH, USA
[2]University of Missouri – Columbia, MS, USA

ABSTRACT

This chapter addresses a phenomenon pertinent to interpersonal hate: enmity. We first review the existing literature relevant to enemies, including a discussion of the relative neglect of this topic and the paucity of research on "the dark side of relationships." The remainder of the chapter addresses definitional, theoretical, and methodological issues in studying enmity. In particular, we provide a novel construct definition of interpersonal enmity in which an enemy is a person someone dislikes; believes is malevolent or threatening; and wishes some degree of social, psychological, or physical harm upon. The benefits of this approach over other conceptualizations are discussed, as are multiple unresolved issues in conceptualizing enmity. The remainder of the chapter discusses future directions for research on enemy relationships including different classes or types of enemies, the integration of enemies with the self, the influence of enmity on person perception, and the role of individual differences in the development of enemy relations. Finally, we argue for the need to move beyond questionnaire and interview

[*] Corresponding author: Psychology Building, Ohio State University, 1835 Neil Avenue, Columbus, OH 43210-1287. E-mail: jones.2333@osu.edu.

methodologies and discuss the benefits which can be obtained by more rigorous hypothesis testing and experimental design in this research area.

INTRODUCTION

As an intensely social species, humans engage in a large and diverse set of interpersonal relationships. At a basic level these relationships are the foundation on which human cooperation, the sharing of resources and information, is built. In fact, our species is so social that this cooperation is utterly necessary for human survival and achievement; that is, humans are *obligately interdependent* (Caporael, 2007). We depend upon one another for survival throughout the lifespan, and ostracism from the group likely meant death throughout much of human evolutionary history. Because of this, human development is characterized by many emergent capacities which serve to maintain positive social relationships (see, e.g., Leary, Tambor, Terdal, & Downs, 1995). Interestingly, these capacities are expressed so early in the lifespan (e.g., by age 1 in some cases; Tomasello, 2007) that they are likely to have a quite substantial genetic component.

In conjunction with our ability to selectively determine with whom relationships form and persist, the basic capacity to cooperate leads most relationships to be positive, providing net benefits to both parties. Evidence exists to support this contention. Consider, for example, that though the impact of marriage on subjective well-being varies with marriage quality, the married are on the whole significantly happier than the unmarried (Diener, Suh, Lucas, & Smith, 1999). The socially isolated, on the other hand, are both psychologically and physically less healthy than those who are more successful in maintaining relationships (Cacioppo & Patrick, 2008).

Against this backdrop, the common phenomenon of interpersonal conflict is somewhat of a puzzle. Obviously, interpersonal relationships characterized by intense dislike, distrust, and malevolence -- in short, by hate -- are not particularly uncommon. Individuals in such relationships are often called enemies. How and why is it that some people come to be enemies? Are certain types of people more likely to form enemies than others? Are there qualitatively different kinds of enmity? Is enmity largely inherent to human nature or are its origins more cultural and institutional? Is enmity pertinent to social problems like aggression and institutional dysfunction? In this chapter, we argue that social psychological science has failed to provide the answers to such critical questions and that the theorizing surrounding such issues is so nascent that investigators have not yet developed an adequate conceptual framework from which to begin formal investigations. Therefore, the focus of the chapter will be offering a novel construct definition of enmity and providing the basic rationale that underlies this conceptual framework. First, however, we address the existence of enmity as a meaningful social phenomenon and review the existing scholarly literature.

Enmity: A Familiar Phenomenon

The word "enemy" is a familiar one in human discourse. It is common to maxims such as *"Know thy enemy"* and *"Keep your friends close and your enemies closer."* When we hear quotations such as Oscar Wilde's *"A man cannot be too careful in his choice of enemies,"* John F. Kennedy's *"Forgive your enemies, but never forget their names,"* or Aesop's *"We often give our enemies the means of our own destruction,"* we easily understand what they mean. As these quotes so clearly indicate, one's enemy is among other things an individual with the capacity to threaten his or her wellbeing. Thus, one should monitor such a person closely.

Some indication that the phenomenon of enmity is common to human experience can be drawn from the field of literature. Enemies are common to classic and contemporary literature, and their conflicts compose much of the most enthralling drama one can experience. One of the authors of this chapter (C. J.) has long found the relationship between Roger Chillingworth and Arthur Dimmesdale in Nathaniel Hawthorne's *The Scarlet Letter* to be particularly memorable. Chillingworth returns from years abroad to find his wife Hester has had a child and will not reveal the father's identity. Upon confirming his suspicions that minister Arthur Dimmesdale is the father, Chillingworth exploits his position as a doctor to augment Arthur's physical and psychological torment (Arthur himself, ashamed, already engaging in intense literal and figurative self-flagellation). The manner in which Chillingworth secretively, methodically, and effectively punishes Arthur for the cuckolding is, so to speak, chilling. If the frequency with which they occur in narrative is any indication, romantic competition and revenge for transgressions, romantic or otherwise, are among the most common bases of enmity. Another is the power struggle. The one between Robin Hood and the Sheriff of Nottingham has captivated audiences in its various forms for centuries. Enemies are, rather obviously, still prominent in contemporary narrative. How many young people cannot name Harry Potter's greatest enemy? (Though, of course, as *Potter* readers know, He Must Not Be Named). Enmity has been a prevalent theme in narrative throughout time, as is apparent in the mythologies that comprise much of humanity's earliest narrative.

A consideration of mythology also highlights the cultural universality of enmity. For example, Ares and Hephaestus of Greek mythology, were made enemies by conflict over the beautiful Aphrodite. In Egyptian mythology, Ra, the sun god, struggled eternally with the monstrous Apep for control of the skies. The Japanese sibling deities Amaterasu and Susanoo had starkly opposing dispositions that continually put them at odds. These are but a few of the relevant examples, and even the most cursory search will easily reveal more. Although successful human cooperation and amity may be the norm, it seems to have made for a less enthralling story than enmity.

Though examples from narrative can be suggestive, the phenomenon must exist outside of fiction to be of interest to psychological science. Numerous historical examples are available, but we will limit ourselves to one of the most notorious. U.S. President Richard Nixon's famed "enemies list" enumerated various individuals and groups seen as obstructing the President's agenda, including politicians and their benefactors, journalists, academics, and celebrities. Compiled by White House Special Counsel Chuck Colson and aides, the existence of the list was revealed at the Watergate hearings by former White House counsel John Dean. Nixon's enemies were to be targeted for government harassment through such mechanisms as IRS audits, denial of grants, and prosecution. For example, in reference to a newspaper article critical of Nixon's close friend, banker Charles Rebozo, Dean said, "I got instructions that one of the authors of the article should have some problems" (Siddon, 1973). The possibility that influential individuals might acquire enemies more easily than others seems likely.

PAST RESEARCH ON ENMITY

In the previous section, we provided evidence that enmity is a meaningful social phenomenon which is common and familiar across time and culture. Of course this evidence was largely indirect and anecdotal, an unfortunate imposition of the current state of the literature. It is simply unknown to psychological science, to the best of our knowledge, how prevalent enmity is because it has never been assessed in large, representative samples. In fact, the sort of interpersonal phenomenon we are referring to as enmity has received little scientific attention in any form. This pronounced shortcoming in the literature has been noted by the few papers which do address the topic (e.g. Adams, 2005; Wiseman & Duck, 1995) and can generally be seen as part of a larger gap in scientific understanding of "the dark side" of interpersonal relationships (see Felmlee & Sprecher, 2000). In particular, Felmlee and Sprecher noted that, "… the process of becoming enemies may be as worthy of study as that of friendship initiation; yet there is no equivalent relationship field of social animosity" (p. 371).

This is not to say that the *word* "enemy" or its variants do not appear in the literature of social psychology or related fields with reference to interpersonal interactions. These concepts are present, but are rarely defined or treated as specific psychological constructs or as the focus of inquiry. Rather, "enemy" is most frequently used as a casual reference to any disliked person. A number of classic social psychological papers are illustrative. For example, Blumberg (1969) wrote, "subjects indicated that they would be happiest not only when their friends liked them, but also when their enemies disliked them" (p. 121). The actual wording of questions posed to participants, however, referred only to how participants would feel about various matched and mismatched levels of liking and never mentioned enemies (or friends). One might expect articles titled "My Enemy's Enemy Is My Friend" (Aronson & Cope, 1968) and "An Observer's Reaction to the Suffering of His Enemy" (Bramel, Taub, & Blum, 1968) to treat the concept more formally. On the contrary, in neither case is it explicitly explained what is meant by the term. In the latter, "enemy" and its variants do not even appear in the main text of the article. We do not mean to criticize these authors or these studies, but merely to illustrate the extent to which the concept of enmity has not had its own distinct identity as a social psychological construct. Interestingly, in both of these studies the "enemy" in question is an experimenter who has been rude to participants. It is not established that participants consider this person an enemy, and it is unclear whether participants plausibly might. Instead, dislike and enmity are equated. While people surely dislike their enemies, we propose that a meaningful construct of enmity should go beyond mere dislike. Unfortunately contemporary usage of the term in psychological discourse continues in this same vague fashion, with a few exceptions noted below.

Contemporary research and theory on enemy relationships can be traced back to Wiseman and Duck (1995), who were the first to formally study such a construct (using the terms "enmity" and "enemyship"). This initial analysis was based on two earlier qualitative studies conducted by Wiseman using an in-depth interview methodology. The first ($N = 80$) concerned friendship, and the second ($N = 60$) concerned enmity. The study pertaining to enmity was constructed such that the questions asked of participants paralleled the previous study of friendship as much as possible. This enabled some comparisons between the two relationship types. Though Wiseman and Duck describe a few parallels between the two sets of data, they conclude that this approach "revealed major differences in the generic aspects of friendship and enemyship. The two kinds of relationships are not two ends of the same continuum, nor are they mirror images of each other—at least in the minds of persons who have experienced these relationships" (p. 46). One difference, for example, is that enemies were described largely in terms of their actions whereas friends were described largely in terms of their enduring characteristics. Because of this dissociation, we have adopted the term "enmity" in the current review in order to avoid implications of equivalence or parallel with the construct of friendship.

The notion of enmity has received some attention in the child and adolescent development literature. Most notably, the journal *New Directions for Child and Adolescent Development* devoted an issue (no. 102, winter 2003) to the topic of antipathy in the relationships of young people. Several of the articles within discuss enemies, though they do so inconsistently with respect to how enmity is conceptualized, and rigorous theorizing of an enmity construct is lacking, as noted in a summary commentary within the special issue (Hartup, 2003). As in the social psychological literature, disliking, mutual disliking, and enmity are not sufficiently distinguished. Be this as it may, many of the empirical findings documented in this literature are intriguing. For example, Card and Hodges (2003) found that while children's attachment styles with their parents were not simple predictors of the propensity to form mutual antipathies, mutual antipathies did tend to form amongst children whose parental attachment styles were incompatible, suggesting that such phenomena must be addressed from a dyadic, relational framework to be fully understood. Parker and Gamm (2003) found that children who were aggressive or lacked social skills were less liked by peers, but this "did not necessarily lead to the accumulation of many mutual enemies" (p. 69). Instead, their data suggested that the tendency towards jealousy was a particularly potent predictor of enmity. Whether such findings generalize to adults or to enmity conceptualized in ways other than mutual disliking is unclear.

Some research has also addressed enmity in a cross-cultural context. Adams (2005), for instance, has argued (and provided preliminary supporting data) that it is more common to have enemies in West African than in American cultures. Moreover, people's views of enmity differ across cultures, such that Americans tend to perceive enmity as rare and pathological. West Africans, however, would consider that view naïve and believe that enemies (including secret enemies), are exceedingly common. These different experiences and conceptions likely vary due to the cultural underpinnings of relationship and self. That is, North American and European self-construals are typically isolated and atomistic, whereas in other cultures, including West African ones, the self is conceived more as a node in an interconnected network of selves (see, e.g., Markus & Kitayama, 1991, on this distinction between "independent" and "interdependent" self-construal). Adams' work suggests that fundamentally different types of enmity, or at the very least different prevailing beliefs about it, exist in different cultures. The construct of enmity described by Wiseman and Duck and the construct analyzed in this chapter, then, pertain more certainly to the enmity experienced and perceived in Western cultures.

Finally, it is necessary to distinguish between enmity at the interpersonal and intergroup levels. The term "enemy" and its variants can apply to either, but they are very different. Interpersonal enmity is based on personal motives and specific experience with a particular individual. Intergroup enmity is based on the motives of the individual-as-group-member and is directed at another solely due to that person's group membership (e.g. in an opposing army). While the former, our focus, is little researched, significantly more attention has been given to the latter phenomenon. Particularly, the notion of "enemy images" in international relations theory is well-known (e.g. Alexander, Brewer, & Hermann, 1999; Silverstein, 1989). It is common to hold stereotyped views of other nations that tend to reflect beliefs about certain attributes and relations. An "enemy" state is one that is powerful and antagonistic. While intergroup enmity is important in its own right, evidence exists to support the contention that it reflects an entirely different phenomenon than the interpersonal one at hand. For example, Holt (1989) explored college students' definitions and images of enemies with respect both to particular individuals and to nations. Interpersonal enemies were those who intended to harm participants or who had betrayed them, and responses indicated that interpersonal enmity had little to do with difference of opinion or ideology. Enemy nations, however, were identified and justified largely on the grounds of oppositional values or policy. Thus, it seems that the ample literature on intergroup conflict should be only tentatively generalized to the less understood domain of interpersonal conflict.

Wiseman and Duck (1995)

At present, the work of Wiseman and Duck (1995) reflects the most substantial theoretical and empirical contribution toward a construct of enmity, and therefore deserves detailed attention. In terms of theory, these authors noted a number of features of enmity observed in the interviews as particularly striking. One was the frequently "unannounced," quality of enmity in which the interpersonal conflict was not entirely open. Another was an increased consciousness and exploitation of power dynamics in these social relationships. It appears that competition for limited resources, including social resources, that provide one with the capacity for influence is often part of the genesis of enmity, and the utilization of acquired power often plays a role in exacerbating it. Wiseman and Duck also described a number of axes along which enemy relationships vary. They identified the *dislike/hate* axis as primary. The intensity of negative affect towards an enemy is likely of great importance. The other two major axes were the *active/passive* and *personal/professional* axes. The former concerns whether a person's enemy is actively engaged in antagonistic actions directed at that person or whether the enemy only possesses a latent capacity to do so. The latter axis concerns the social domain in which the relationship is rooted. Variance along these axes is likely to be important in understanding enmity, particularly in predicting how one will manage the challenge of enmity. At present, however, exactly what consequences follow from such variance remains a very open question. Other axes designated as "less important," though it is not apparent on what grounds, were the *close/distant contact* and *aware/unaware* axes. The former concerns the extent to which contact with the enemy is inevitable, and the latter concerns one's certainty about the presence or degree of malicious intent held by the enemy. Finally, *time frame*, or temporal distance, is likely of some consequence.

Although the extensive interviews conducted by Wiseman provide a rich source of information, very little quantitative analysis of this data has been communicated. Nevertheless, some of the empirical findings can be described in broad strokes. First, only a "small percentage of respondents claimed they had no enemies" (p. 48). Enemies tended to emerge from the realms of personal social activity and professional life -- they found no indication of enmity within families (but see Adams, 2005). They noted that individuals virtually never cited their own behavior in the development of enmity, almost certainly reflecting a self-serving attributional bias. That is, participants saw enmity as originating from specific and unanticipated acts by the other party -- betrayals, disappointments, embarrassments, attacks, and the like. Based on the interview content, it appears likely that many enemies are competitors or rivals. Many enemies were also once considered friends. Contexts promoting conflict over limited resources, jealousy, and power struggle were seen as facilitative of enmity. Once acquired, enemies engendered feelings of frustration and disgust, though the primary response enemies elicited may have been avoidance. Many sought social support in dealing with enemies, and relatively few reported intent to attack or retaliate against enemies.

DEFINING ENMITY: A WAY FORWARD

So far, we have avoided defining enmity because the matter requires considerable attention. As the previous literature review demonstrates, the term can take on a number of distinct meanings. Often, psychologists do not specify exactly what is meant by the term. Defining enmity, however, is of critical importance for it is only with a clear and unambiguous definition that predictions and theory can be adequately communicated and corresponding operationalizations can be developed. As noted above, such efforts have been rare.

First, let us examine how enmity has been previously defined. Wiseman and Duck (1995) were the first to extensively discuss a construct of enmity *as a relationship*. They refrain, however, from concisely defining the term. Adams (2005), citing Wiseman and Duck, defines it thusly: "a personal relationship of hatred and malice in which one person desires another person's downfall or attempts to sabotage another person's progress" (p. 948). This fairly captures the gist of the construct as articulated by Wiseman and Duck, and it is surely evocative of the phenomenon in question. However, as a formal definition (to be fair, it was likely not intended as such), it is problematic. In order to be clearly specified, the terms used to define enmity should themselves be clearly specified psychological constructs with conventional, consensually accepted meanings. To define enmity with terms such as "hatred" and "progress" is to beg the question of what these terms themselves mean. Hate, as this volume makes clear, is not a simple construct with a conventional usage. Is hate best conceptualized as the extreme negative end of a liking continuum? Or, is hate somehow qualitatively distinct from dislike? For instance, some might conceptualize hate as an emotional construct, complete with distinctive physiological manifestation. Some identify hate as special in the sense that hated things are those bad objects to be approached and destroyed, rather than avoided. One can say she hates beets or hates, say, her boss and mean very different things. If enmity is to be defined by hate, the intended meaning of hate must be articulated. "Downfall" is similarly unspecified but seems to exclude as an enemy anyone who desires less than the total ruination of another -- a boundary condition that seems inappropriate given the data of Wiseman and Duck (1995). "Sabotage" has a strong connotation suggesting covertness, implying that one who is overtly adversarial does not qualify. In sum, though the definition above is evocative, it is not an adequate formal construct definition because it is too unclear and, taken literally, inadequately inclusive. Thus, it would pose problems of operationalization. These same problems are common to standard dictionary definitions of enemy and its variants.

Enmity has also rarely been operationalized. Some research has identified enemies by reciprocal dislike, that is, each party endorses a negative attitude toward the other on a scale item or items (e.g. Card & Hodges, 2003). Though this is a perfectly straightforward and useful method, it is obviously a more direct and face valid operationalization of mutual antipathy rather than enmity per se. This is clearly a related construct, but the two are not, in our view, synonymous (see Abecassis, 2003 for one conceptualization relating the two constructs). Other research which has had to operationalize enmity typically involves simply asking participants about their enemies. Clearly, this is problematic because it leaves much to the vicissitudes of interpretation by participants and likely taps various phenomena that could (and should) be distinguished at a construct level.

Enmity: A Tripartite Definition

We offer here a definition of enmity that shares much of the spirit of other definitions of enmity as a relationship, but is phrased in terms of clear psychological constructs more suitable for future operationalization. An individual's enemy is a person whom the individual: a) dislikes b) perceives as malevolent, and c) wishes harm upon. The first component is attitudinal, referring to a summary evaluation associated in memory with that person (see Fazio, 1995). Thus, thinking about or encountering the enemy will activate negative evaluative processes (see Cacioppo & Berntson, 1994 on the substrates of negativity and its independence from positivity). This activation of basic negativity then serves as a building block for more complex and differentiated feelings and emotions like anger or disgust (Russell, 2003). The second component is more specific and cognitive in nature. By malevolent we mean that the individual perceives the enemy as unjustifiably threatening or harmful in prior behavior, character, or intent. Finally, an enemy is someone upon whom one hopes some kind of psychological, social, or physical harm, meant in the broadest sense possible. To be clear, one need not necessarily intend or desire to personally harm one's enemy. It is instead sufficient that one wishes some form of suffering, retribution, or psychological discomfort upon this individual. Thus, one may or may not actively harm one's enemy. The critical difference between an enemy and a merely disliked individual is that one prefers bad things to happen to an enemy because of the enemy's malevolence, something that is not the case for all disliked individuals. One hopes the enemy does not achieve his or her goals, one would be less likely to intervene to prevent harm from befalling an enemy, and one would likely react less unfavorably to observing the pain of an enemy (cf. Bramel, Taub, & Blum, 1968).

We view each of these three components as a necessary but not sufficient condition of enmity. That is, in the absence of any of these components, the case would seem to lack essential characteristics of the enemy relationship. Thus, any one component alone would not suffice to constitute enmity. Although each must be present for an enemy relationship to form, we do not conceptualize enmity as a dichotomous (present vs. absent) construct. Instead, we view the degree of enmity as continuous. Each component can differ in intensity with the degree of enmity varying as a function of these combined intensities. Weak enmity might reflect all three components but not intensely: for example, one might hope an annoying coworker viewed as egotistical and overly competitive be passed over for promotion. On the other hand, strong enmity might be formed towards a despised individual who has seriously and wantonly hurt a loved one and is viewed as deserving the harshest of punishments. This conceptualization has the advantage of being easily quantifiable (i.e. each component can be straightforwardly measured and combined with the others), though how this might be done *optimally* is a question best left aside pending further theoretical and empirical advances.

On the Tripartite Nature of Enmity

Although the three components of enmity are each distinct constructs which contribute separately to the meaning of enmity, various psychological processes exist that will cause the components to influence one another. For example, because of the motivation for cognitive consistency that many have argued are basic to human psychology (Festinger, 1957; Heider, 1958), a general trend towards the coherence of affect, cognition, and behavior is to be expected. More specifically, a host of specific processes relate each component to the others. We will provide some illustrative examples.

First, simply disliking another individual is likely to foster negative beliefs about and hope for harm to befall this person. Some recent work provides especially compelling evidence in this regard. Miele, Todd, and Richeson (2009) used a subliminal evaluative conditioning procedure to associate negative affect with unfamiliar groups. After this, participants reported the extent to which they believed each group possessed certain qualities. Interestingly, individuals spontaneously generated beliefs about the groups consistent with the feelings that had been subliminally attached to them. Negative evaluations can also produce unfavorable cognitions due to their biasing effects on subsequent information processing. For instance, information about a disliked person is likely to be elaborated in a biased fashion, such that even a set of evaluatively varied but objectively neutral information about a disliked individual will foster more negative beliefs and a more extremely negative attitude (Lord, Ross, & Lepper, 1979). Information that pertains unfavorably to the disliked individual will be accepted unquestioningly while information that pertains favorably will be scrutinized harshly. In addition, disliking a person, or even expecting to do so (Kelley, 1950), will produce biased hypothesis testing about that individual's character, motives, and the like. Looking for negatives will allow individuals to more easily identify this information, and the motivation to view the person negatively will produce a lower threshold for evidence that confirms this hypothesis (and correspondingly raise the threshold of evidence for disconfirming hypotheses; Ditto & Lopez, 1992; Pyszczynski & Greenberg, 1987). Research has also demonstrated that simple dislike can actually cause an individual not only to wish harm upon another but also to become more likely to act upon that desire (see the General Aggression Model; Anderson & Bushman, 2002). In particular, negative affect in the form of pain, frustration, and anger are especially likely to elicit such aggressive tendencies.

One's negative beliefs concerning the threat and malevolence of another are likely to produce increased dislike and the desire to see that individual come to harm. Both general evaluations (Smith, Bruner, & White, 1956) and emotional experiences (Russell, 2003; Scherer, Schorr, & Johnstone, 2001) are shaped by cognitive appraisals of objects and situations. Further, the more frequently one elaborates on such beliefs, which can form the basis of a negative attitude, the more one's attitude is likely to be rehearsed, thus coming to mind more readily on future occasions (Powell & Fazio, 1984). Rumination, the tendency to repeatedly and prolongedly think about negative experiences and feelings, has been linked to aggressive tendencies (Anderson & Bushman, 2002; Anestis, Anestis, Selby, & Joiner, 2009). Thus, much research suggests that when thinking about how an individual is threatening or malevolent, both dislike of that individual and behavioral tendencies toward aggression against that individual (a relatively strong manifestation of the desire for harm to befall a person) will increase.

Finally, although somewhat less intuitively obvious, one's desire for harm to befall another (or actually harming another) can also produce corresponding dislike and negative beliefs. This is because such thoughts (or actions) are likely to produce a sense of discomfort that threatens people's tendency to view themselves as good and moral beings. Therefore, self-justification processes serving to restore one's positive self-conception are likely to follow. One manner of doing so would be to increase the extent to which the person is viewed as disliked and deserving of harm (i.e., derogation). Tavris and Aronson (2007) extensively describe such self-justification processes and have shown that people are especially likely to derogate another after having performed a hurtful action towards this individual. Though to our knowledge it has not been demonstrated that merely wishing harm upon another provokes such self-justificatory tendencies, to the extent these desires threaten one's self-image, there is every reason to expect that it does. In sum, a host of processes lead dislike, perceptions of malevolence, and the desire for harm to feed into one another to produce an integrated, self-perpetuating tri-partite enmity. This feedback and crosstalk between the three components are likely what make enmity such a strong and persistent relationship that can be immune to various reconciliation efforts (Wiseman & Duck, 1995).

Therefore, the appearance or augmentation of any one component of enmity is likely to foster the appearance or augmentation of the others. We do not mean to say, however, that the mere presence of any one component will inexorably facilitate the formation of tripartite enmity. This would not necessarily be the case partly because causal links between the components that we have described are contingent upon the frequency with which the individual is encountered or thought about. Further, the likelihood that one component will influence the others obviously depends on the strength or intensity of that component. It is clearly possible for one to dislike a person without perceiving that person as malevolent, to wish someone harm without disliking that person (likely for some utilitarian reason), and so on. We predict, however, that full-blown enmity often follows when any particular component emerges to a strong degree and the individual cannot henceforth be easily avoided.

OTHER ISSUES IN THE DEFINITION OF ENMITY

Mutuality and Directionality

Two related conceptual aspects of enmity relating to some of the above definitional issues are the ideas of mutuality and directionality. In some relationships, individuals may harbor roughly equivalent antipathies in form and degree, and often these are the examples that are evoked upon mention of enemies. The enmity is mutual. Some dictionary definitions even go so far as to define enmity as such. However, the existing literature points to clear asymmetries in the enmity individuals describe (Wiseman & Duck, 1995) and the existence of "secret" enemies (Adams, 2005) is particularly inconsistent with this definition. Thus, although the proportion of enemies that are mutual remains unknown, we see no reason to limit the construct to these cases. Consider our first literary example. Roger Chillingworth of *The Scarlet Letter* hides his full identity and knowledge from Arthur Dimmesdale, which allows him to punish Dimmesdale all the more effectively. Arthur, on the other hand, bears no ill-will whatsoever towards Chillingworth, at least while the ruse persisted. By our definition, Chillingworth's enemy was Dimmesdale, but not vice versa. The enmity was not mutual, and yet the example, at least in our view, clearly reflects an example of an enemy relationship.

The prior example raises the issue of directionality. Note that the earlier definition we described refers to one person hating and desiring another's downfall and is flexible with respect to the issue of directionality. One might say that two people are enemies if one or the other feels a certain way. This raises a potential terminological and communicative problem. If one says "Chris' enemy," it may refer, to be concise, either to someone who Chris hates or to someone who hates Chris. One solution would be to introduce terminology that distinguishes the two. For example, the Latin prefixes *ad* and *ab*, meaning toward or away from a point of reference respectively could be utilized. Thus, Chris' (the point of reference) ad-enemy hates Chris. Chris' ab-enemy is one whom Chris hates. Another solution to this communicative problem is to specify directionality in the definition as we have done. Chris' enemy, using our definition, is one who Chris dislikes, perceives as malevolent and wishes harm upon. To say "Chris' enemy" does not necessarily imply anything about this other person's feelings etc. about Chris, though if one were to say Chris and another are enemies, the implication would be that the feelings are mutual.

The disadvantage of this approach is that it is at odds with individuals' tendency to focus disproportionately on *the other* when describing their enemies. Individuals, asked about their enemies, tend to focus on the hatred and ill will directed at themselves. However, there is a strong pragmatic reason for defining enemy as *from* a point of reference. When measuring enmity using our conceptualization, one must ask individuals about dislike, beliefs, and intent to harm. One can answer these questions about themselves or about others. The degree of knowledge and certainty participants can have is much greater in the former case, which is how measurement would occur focusing on enmity directed *from* the participant. Although individuals are frequently biased and are particularly unaware of their own biases (Pronin, Gilovich, & Ross, 2004), these biases tend to be self-serving. If an individual reports disliking another, perceiving that person as malevolent, and desiring that they are harmed, we can be quite certain it is true. When a participant must report whether such things are true of another, measurement of enmity is likely to be much less reliable.

Intimacy, Familiarity, and Longevity

Another definitional issue is that of intimacy or familiarity. In conceiving enmity within the domain of personal relationships, we are specifying that a minimum degree of intimacy or familiarity is met. The conflict generates from dynamics particular to the two individuals and their interactions rather than group memberships or the actions of the individuals' affiliates. Others may be involved, but the sentiments are specific to the two parties. One might go further and define enmity as a phenomenon *within* close groups (e.g. Adams & Dzokoto, 2007). Depending on how stringently an in-group context is defined, this would seem to exclude many relationships from the domain of enmity. For example, one of the authors has a friend who owns a business. He has what we would consider an enemy. This enemy is a business rival who provides roughly the same service and competes for customers. In this friend's case, at the most meaningful level of self-identification, the enemy is from an outgroup (the other company). Though it is not irrelevant to their relationship that their groups are opposed, it happens to be in this case that the enmity is largely rooted specifically in interpersonal interactions and perceptions. Not all members of that group are his enemies and it was the unique actions of this particular outgroup member that created the dislike, perceptions of malevolence, and desire for harm. Because of this, we view this case as one that should fall within the theoretical domain of interpersonal enmity. There is, however, an empirical question at hand. Is enmity within a close ingroup similar to enmity between individuals in different groups? Or are these two forms sufficiently dissimilar that they ought to be differentiated at a construct level? It is likely too soon to say, but we do not see any reason at present to limit the construct to intragroup relationships.

Defining enmity as a relationship means that we typically have had direct interaction with our enemies and have a relatively high degree of familiarity with them. As with other relationships, this suggests a certain degree of longevity. Thus, the two individuals in question will likely have prolonged contact and the elements of enmity have persisted over time. However, some special cases that vary from this prototype must be considered. Some individuals, in particular those who are public figures and/or are particularly influential, might have enemies who they know *of* but with whom they may never have had any actual direct contact.

Nixon and his enemies come to mind. The problem of the public figure is interesting because another person might paradoxically know the public figure very well and not at all, simultaneously. More generally, one can be influenced in a negative way by another who is almost completely unknown but still come to consider that individual as an enemy. Another special case involves relationships that are highly context-dependent. A football player, for example, might identify an opposing player as particularly noxious and a ripe target for harm, yet this sentiment might dissolve at game's end. At this early stage, we again view more inclusive definitions as prudent, though it may prove superior to restrict the construct to particular types or degrees of intimacy and longevity as more is learned.

FUTURE DIRECTIONS

Typology

As has been alluded to repeatedly, it is possible that the construct of enmity can be further differentiated. Differences in enemy relationships obviously exist, and it may be the case that some differences are consistently produced by sufficiently distinct circumstances and/or consistently lead to sufficiently distinct outcomes that it would prove theoretically useful to specify subtypes of enmity in addition to identifying more isolated continua of variability of enmity. Determining whether such unique kinds of enmity exist is an important problem for future research. The personal/professional axis identified by Wiseman and Duck (1995) is a particularly interesting potential source of differentiation because of its more qualitative nature (compared to the other axes they identified as important). The dominant emotions that an enemy evokes might also be integral to differentiating the construct of enmity. Different emotions are known to arise from different antecedents, to differ experientially, and to promote different behaviors. An enemy that primarily evokes fear is likely to be very different than one that particularly evokes anger, disgust, or jealousy. All of this, obviously, remains speculative.

The Self

Clearly, relationships are extremely important aspects of people's lives. One primary manner in which individuals self-identify is through their important relationships with others (relational identities -- Brewer & Gardner, 1996), such as one's identity as spouse, parent, sibling, boss, partner, etc. In close relationships, a merging of self and other can occur. This is not a mere turn of phrase; at the level of mental representation, close others can become so closely associated with the self that the two are represented in memory in an overlapping fashion such that activation of one activates the other (Aron, Aron, Tudor, & Nelson, 1991). Conceivably, relationships with one's enemies might come to possess a similar significance. This is especially likely when the enemy relationship is so intense that two individuals are engaged in active and significant attempts to cause harm to one another over a prolonged period. When this is the case, one may begin to define oneself as a person whose purpose in life is, to a substantial extent, to successfully oppose the enemy. To the extent that this occurs, the destruction of an enemy or resolution of enmity may come to pose problems of self-identification. The newly impoverished self-concept may involve the person struggling to determine who he or she is and what his or her goals should be (cf. Nord, 1997). Although such intense enmity is probably relatively rare, such relationships do appear in literature. Though in reality one's enemy is unlikely to be an animal, to say the least, Captain Ahab's single-minded, self-consuming quest to destroy Moby Dick, the whale who bit off his leg, comes to mind.

Person Perception and Enmity

People surely perceive and process information about their enemies in a different manner than they do other people. In particular, individuals are likely to exhibit two separate tendencies that will interact to produce a unique form of person perception. As described above, the first of these tendencies will be a negative bias in the processing of information -- people will process information about their enemies in an extremely biased manner, altering the type of attributions made about their behaviors and the perceived consequences of their actions. This will tend to result in perceiving the enemy as having more negative characteristics, having more suspect motivations, and as generally being just *worse* than would be seen by a more neutral observer. Especially when enemies are strongly disliked, people will be motivated to perceive them in the worst possible way, and this bias may cause them to quite literally see their enemies more negatively than other people (see Balcetis & Dunning, 2006 for a discussion of higher-order motivational influence on lower-order perception).

At the same time, however, a powerful accuracy motive is also likely to be present. Because of the threat that enemies pose, one has a vested interest in being able to accurately judge an enemy's capacities and predict an enemy's actions. Especially for enemies with whom one has a high degree of contact, the malevolent enemy must be scrutinized and anticipated. This will likely motivate individuals to commit a great deal of their information processing resources to the enemy whenever this individual is present in addition to ruminating about the person in absentia. Such increased attention combined with bias likely makes individuals particularly adept at identifying their enemies' shortcomings and weaknesses, though they may be prone to exaggerating them. Interestingly, committing such a large amount of cognitive attention to this single individual is likely to produce a deficit in the processing of other information in the environment when an enemy is present or on the mind. By serving as a cognitive load, the presence of an enemy is likely to produce a variety of information processing outcomes related to reduced mental capacity (e.g., Biernat, Kobrynowicz, & Weber, 2003; Reeder, 1997; Spears, Haslam, & Jansen, 1999; Van Knippenberg, Dijksterhuis, & Vermeulen, 1999). This interplay between strong bias, increased elaboration, and accuracy constraints imposed by the need to predict the enemy creates an intriguing dynamic of person perception.

Individual Differences

Various individual differences surely play a role in enmity. Some attention has been paid to gender, leading to the conclusion that same-sex versus cross-sex enmities differ systematically (see Wiseman & Duck, 1995 and the previously mentioned special issue of *New Directions for Adolescent and Child Development*). Gender differences in the propensities for physical and social aggression are also pertinent to nature of the harm component of enmity (see Anderson & Bushman, 2002; Archer & Coyne, 2005). Demographic variables such as political affiliation and religiosity may relate to enmity. A host of personality variables may also relate with enmity in various ways. The basic fundamental factors of personality, such as the Big-5 or HEXACO, seem an appropriate place to start testing for relationships. Also, narcissism, psychopathy, and Machivellianism -- the so-called dark triad of personality -- are especially likely to affect one's propensity to make enemies and the methods selected to deal with them.

Methodology

As mentioned, the most notable research on enmity has involved interview methodologies. This largely qualitative approach is quite suitable for initial inquiry into the phenomenon. Given the paucity of research on this topic, it is likely that further research in this vein will continue to be useful. Additionally, however, it is of utmost importance that researchers begin to investigate enmity in other ways that allow for more precise quantification of variables. In particular, experimental methodologies in which an independent variable is manipulated are crucial to establishing causal relationships pertinent to enmity. Scenario methodologies would seem to lend themselves rather readily to such early investigations. In particular, it would be relatively simple to manipulate variables relating to the setting of a relationship, the behavior of the enemy, etc., and examine how participants expect they would feel and behave, the degree to which the components of enmity would be met, and the like. Of course scenario methodologies are problematic because they rely heavily on introspection, but findings from scenario studies could be bolstered with other more intensive methods including the interview and behavioral studies. Ultimately, it will be necessary to create enemies in the laboratory, perhaps using paradigms like those in classic research involving rude, insulting experimenters (e.g. Aronson & Cope, 1968; Bramel, Taub, & Blum, 1968). Of course due to both practical and ethical constraints, it will probably only prove feasible to create weak enemies in the laboratory, and these would lack the characteristic of being particularly meaningful social relationships. The potential payoff in knowledge from experimental methodologies involving the creation of enmity in the laboratory, however, is enormous because of the degree of control it affords.

Enmity has also, to date, only been studied in small, convenient samples. Much could be learned from the use of large, representative samples that could reveal the contours of the phenomenon in a more definitive manner than has yet occurred. Another sampling issue concerns the possibility of studying both parties in enemy relationships simultaneously. While this poses a substantial logistical challenge, the dyadic nature of the phenomenon demands it. Both field and laboratory contexts could potentially be utilized towards this aim.

CONCLUSION

Enmity is a recognizable phenomenon in the social world, one that most everyone has observed if not experienced. Somehow, however, it has gone mostly unstudied by the field to which it perhaps most directly pertains, social psychology. At present, a clearly articulated construct of enmity has yet to be developed. Towards this end, we have offered a novel construct definition. Enmity is a social relationship in which one dislikes one's enemy, perceives one's enemy as malevolent, and desires some sort of physical, psychological, or social harm to befall this person. This tripartite definition is easily operationalized and makes a number of novel predictions regarding the antecedents and consequences of enmity. The existing literature points to various ways in which enmity might be further differentiated or specified as a construct. The extent to which this area remains open is daunting. Nevertheless, many points of departure are quite clear, both respect to theory and method. Advancing along these lines will not only prove informative for understanding this manifestation of human relationship but should also provide a great deal of insight into a variety of practical social problems, such as interpersonal aggression and hate.

REFERENCES

Abecassis, M. (2003). I hate you just the way you are: Exploring the formation, maintenance, and need for enemies. *New Directions for Child and Adolescent Development, 102*, 5-22.

Adams, G. (2005). The cultural grounding of personal relationship: Enemyship in North American and West African Worlds. *Journal of Personality and Social Psychology, 88*, 948-68.

Adams, G. & Dzokoto, V. A. (2007). Genital-shrinking panic in Ghana: A cultural psychological analysis. *Culture & Psychology, 13*, 83-104.

Alexander, M. G., Brewer, M. B. & Herrmann, R. K. (1999). Images and affect: a functional analysis of out-group stereotypes. *Journal of Personality and Social Psychology, 77*, 78-93.

Anderson, C. A. & Bushman, B. J. (2002). Human aggression. *Annual Review of Psychology, 53*, 27-51.

Anestis, M. D., Anestis, J. C., Selby, E. A. & Joiner, T. E. (2009). Anger rumination across forms of aggression. *Personality and Individual Differences, 46*, 192-196.

Aron, A., Aron, E. N., Tudor, M. & Nelson, G. (1991). Close relationships as including other in the self. *Journal of Personality and Social Psychology, 60,* 241-253.

Aronson, E. & Cope, V. (1968). My enemy's enemy is my friend. *Journal of Personality and Social Psychology, 8,* 8-12.

Balcetis, E. & Dunning, D. See what you want to see: Motivational influences on visual perception. *Journal of Personality and Social Psychology, 91,* 612-625.

Biernat, M., Kobrynowicz, D. & Weber, D. (2003). Stereotypes and shifting standards: Some paradoxical effects of cognitive load. *Journal of Applied Social Psychology, 33,* 2060-2079.

Blumberg, H. H. (1969). On being liked more than you like. *Journal of Personality and Social Psychology, 11,* 121-128.

Bramel, D., Taub, B. & Blum, B. (1968). An observer's reaction to the suffering of his enemy. *Journal of Personality and Social Psychology, 8,* 384-392.

Brewer, M. B. & Gardner, W. (1996). Who is this "We"? Levels of collective identity and self representations. *Journal of Personality and Social Psychology, 71,* 83-93.

Cacioppo, J. T. & Berntson, G. G. (1994). Relationship between attitudes and evaluative space: A critical review with emphasis on the separability of positive and negative substrates. *Psychological Bulletin, 115,* 401-423.

Cacioppo, J. T. & Patrick, W. (2008). *Loneliness: Human nature and the need for social connection.* New York: Norton.

Caporael, L. R. (2007). Evolutionary theory for social and cultural psychology. In A. Kruglanski & E. T. Higgins (Eds.) *Social Psychology: Handbook of Basic Principles,* 2nd ed. (3- 18). New York: Guildford.

Card, N. A. & Hodges, E. V. E. (2003). Parent-child relationships and enmity withpeers: The role of avoidant and preoccupied attachment. *New Directions for Child and Adolescent Development, 102,* 23-37.

Diener, E., Suh, E. M., Lucas, R. E. & Smith, H. L. (1999). Subjective well-being: Three decades of progess. *Psychological Bulletin, 125,* 276-302.

Ditto, P. H. & Lopez, D. F. (1992). Motivated skepticism: Use of differential decision criteria for preferred and nonpreferred conclusions. *Journal of Personality and Social Psychology, 63,* 568-584.

Fazio, R. H. (1995). Attitudes as object-evaluation associations: Determinants, consequences, and correlates of attitude accessibility. In R. E. Petty & Krosnick, J. A. (Eds.) *Attitude strength: Antecedents and consequences.* Hillsdale, NJ: Erlbaum.

Felmlee, D. & Sprecher, S. (2000). Close relationships and social psychology: Intersections and future paths. *Social Psychology Quarterly, 63,* 365-376.

Festinger, L. (1957). *A theory of cognitive dissonance.* Stanford, CA: Stanford UP.

Hartup, W. W. (2003). Toward understanding mutual antipathies in childhood and adolescence. *New Directions for Child and Adolescent Development, 102*, 111-123.

Heider, F. (1958). *The psychology of interpersonal relations.* New York: Wiley.

Holt, R. R. (1989). College students' definitions and images of enemies. *Journal of Social Issues, 45*, 33-50.

Kelley, H. H. (1950). The warm-cold variable in first impressions of persons. *Journal of Personality, 18,* 431-439.

Leary, M. R., Tambor, E. S., Terdal, S. K. & Downs, D. L. (1995). Self-esteem as an interpersonal monitor: The sociometer hypothesis. *Journal of Personality and Social Psychology, 68*, 518-530.

Lord, C. G., Ross, L. & Lepper, M. R. (1979). Biased assimilation and attitude polarization: The effects of prior theories on subsequently considered evidence. *Journal of Personality and Social Psychology, 11*, 2098-2109.

Markus, H. R. & Kitayama, S. (1991). Culture and the self: Implications for cognition, emotion, and motivation. *Psychological Review, 98*, 224-253.

Miele, D. B., Todd, A. R. & Richeson, J. A. (2009, February). Stereotypes out of thin air. The effect of negative emotions on perceptions of novel outgroups. Paper presented at the Annual Meeting of the Society for Personality and *Social Psychology*, Tampa, FL.

Nord, D. (1997). Threats to identity in survivors of multiple AIDS-related losses. *American Journal of Psychotherapy, 51*, 387.

Parker, J. G. & Gamm, B. K. (2003). Describing the dark side of preadolescents' peer experiences: Four questions (and data) on preadolescents' enemies. *New Directions for Child and Adolescent Development, 102*, 55-72.

Powell, M. C. & Fazio, R. H. (1984). Attitude accessibility as a function of repeated attitudinal expression. *Personality and Social Psychology Bulletin, 10*, 139-148.

Pronin, E., Gilovich, T. & Ross, L. (2004). Objectivity in the eye of the beholder: Divergent perceptions of bias in self versus others. *Psychological Review, 111*, 781-799.

Pyszczynski, T. & Greenberg, J. (1987). Toward an integration of cognitive and motivational perspectives on social inference: A biased hypothesis-testing model. In L. Berkowitz (Eds.) *Advances in experimental social psychology* (*Vol. 20*, 297-340). San Diego, Ca: Academic Press.

Reeder, G. D. (1997). Dispositional inferences of ability: content and process. *Journal of Experimental Social Psychology, 33,* 171–189.

Russell, J. A. (2003). Core affect and the psychological construction of emotion. *Psychological Review, 110,* 145-172.

Scherer, K. R., Schorr, A. & Johnstone, T. (Eds.) *Appraisal processes in emotion: Theory, methods, research.* Oxford: Oxford UP.

Siddon, A. (1973, June 27). Dean tells of "enemy list" kept by White House staff. *Chicago Tribune,* 1.

Silverstein, B. (1989). Enemy images: The psychology of U.S. attitudes and cognition regarding the Soviet Union. *American Psychologist, 44,* 903-913.

Smith, M. B., Bruner, J. S. & White, R. W. (1956). *Opinions and personality.* New York: Wiley.

Spears, R., Haslam, S. A. & Jansen, R. (1999). The effect of cognitive load on social categorization in the category confusion paradigm. *European Journal of Social Psychology ,* 29, 621-639.

Tavris, C. & Aronson, E. (2007). *Mistakes were made (but not by me): Why we justify foolish beliefs, bad decisions, and hurtful acts.* New York: Harcourt.

Tomasello, M. (2007). Cooperation and communication in the 2nd year of life. *Child Development Perspectives, 1,* 8-12.

Van Knippenberg, A., Dijksterhuis, A. & Vermeulen, D. (1999). Judgment and memory of a criminal act: the effects of stereotypes and cognitive load. *European Journal of Social Psychology, 29,* 191-201.

Wiseman, J. P. & Duck, S. (1995). Having and managing enemies: A very challenging relationship. In S. Duck and J. T. Wood (Eds.) *Confronting relationship challenges* (43-72). Thousand Oaks, CA: Sage.

In: Psychology of Hate   ISBN: 978-1-61668-050-3
Editors: Carol T. Lockhardt, pp.59-81   © 2010 Nova Science Publishers, Inc.

Chapter 3

HATE, REVENGE AND FORGIVENESS: A HEALTHY, EGO-STRENGTHENING ALTERNATIVE TO THE EXPERIENCE OF OFFENSE

Patrick F. Cioni

Private Practice of Counseling and Psychotherapy,
Scranton, Pennsylvania, USA

ABSTRACT

Forgiveness is a choice, a process and an internal response that involves release of negative affect including anger which, when chronic, can develop into hatred. It is not forgetting or condoning, and it does not necessarily lead to reconciliation though that is potentiated. The process of forgiveness includes 1) re-constructuring cognitions about the offender and self and 2) re-imaging the offender and re-experiencing self and violator. This object transformation results in ego development since objects and object constellations are the building blocks of ego identity (Kernberg, 1984). The ego is empowered to more effectively deal with conflict and associated negative affect due to abatement of anger and decreased internal arousal. This increases the ego's ability for effective communication and conflict resolution.

Stages of forgiveness and gradated cognitions typical of each stage are identified. Each forgiveness stage includes increasingly efficacious cognitions which exemplify a process of cognitive upleveling and ego strengthening. The distinction between forgiveness and reconciliation is important. Forgiveness is an intrapersonal event or process which potentiates but does not necessitate a behavioral coming together, while reconciliation is interpersonal and involves a behavioral encounter. Reconciliation involves risk-taking behavior which can become less threatening to the individual with increasing forgiveness and growing ego strength.

INTRODUCTION

Forgiveness is a choice, a "punctilious event" in time, or a "critical moment of commitment," and an on-going process in the instance of serious violation. (Cunningham, 1985, p. 146). Forgiveness involves "moments of grace...coming unexpectedly as a gift...not of one's own making..." (Bauer, et al, 1992, P. 157). Forgiveness is essentially a gift from God to the human community for distinct and specific purposes, one being the restoration of personal and communal health (Bauer et al, 1992; Enright & Zell, 1989; Ferch, 1998; Ritzman, 1987).

Personal and relational functioning can be threatened by serious offense. Violation frequently results in anger with associated inner tension and obsessive thought. A vengeful attitude can be followed by aggressive fixation on the object of the offender. The desire for revenge results in tension reduction but only temporarily, since the object-image is not destroyed or amiably transformed. Experience of satisfaction by means of revenge is impermanent and deceptive. Forgiveness can eventually make the object non-threatening and bring about permanent tension reduction.

The sequence of intrapersonal events in revenge can be summarized as follows:

1. A violation occurs.
2. Negative emotions follow; these can include anger, fear, frustration, hurt, disappointment.
3. The associated idea, conscious and/or unconscious, can be such as "I'll get even."
4. Negative emotions persist.
5. The object-image changes form: from friend to enemy.
6. An aggression-energy charge (cathexis) is fixedly directed at the object, producing inner conflict. Fixation puts an end to the instinct's mobility (Freud, 1915) and makes the processing of anger difficult or impossible.

In forgiveness, it is hypothesized that the violator's object-representation is transformed from hated and feared to accepted (Hunter, 1978) and healthier (Vitz & Mango, 1997a), and the juxtaposed sequence is:

1. Violation.
2. Negative emotions.
3. The informed ego consciously makes a cognitive intervention: "I choose to forgive this person."
4. Negative emotions are eventually alleviated.
5. The object-image is less threatening or remains non-threatening. If a change from friendly to hostile image has begun, such transformation is eventually ended.
6. De-cathexis of an increasingly permanent type ensues. Fixation is curtailed or prevented; a peaceful inner state can follow.

PURPOSES OF HATE

"(T)he aim (of hatred) is not to eliminate but maintain the relationship with the hated object so as to torture it" (Vitz & Mango, 1997b p. 67); hatred enables the person to "keep the object and make it suffer pain..." (ibid). Vitz & Mango (1997b, pp. 69-70) point out that hatred as a pathological defense mechanism can, additionally, serve the ego in numerous ways:

1. Hatred can be used as "an unconscious defense against painful memories and affect."
2. Hate can be "used to protect oneself from being vulnerable" in a close relationship.
3. "(H)atred almost always involves splitting. It keeps one from recognizing that one's self is seriously flawed and that others (who have offended) also have positive attributes."
4. Hatred can be "a form of self-indulgent laziness...the hated person is responsible for one's failures."
5. "(F)eelings of moral superiority are probably the most frequently observed rewards of hatred. Hatred and revenge...make people feel alive and powerful. The pleasure of revenge in fantasy or fact is a common theme in literature and the media. Because of positive rewards deriving

from hatred, it's not surprising that forgiveness is viewed by many people as weakness; as a giving up of power" (Vitz & Mango, 1997b, p.70).

FORGIVENESS: DIFFICULTIES, DESCRIPTIONS AND PURPOSES

When the offense is deep and painful and hatred has developed, the desire to retaliate is typically strong. Pingleton (1997, p. 404) describes the lex talionis, the law of the talon (Exod. 21:24; JB), as "the organism's universal, reflexive propensity for retaliation and retribution in the face of hurt or pain at the hand of another." In choosing forgiveness, a person opposes his or her own desires, thoughts, feelings, memories and associations, all of which propel the person in the direction of wounding the wounder. A natural impulse drives the violated individual to act against the violator, and his or her inner image, to avenge and restore a sense of safety and power to the wounded ego.

Forgiveness offends the ego which seeks to protect and defend against the experience of violation. "Even for good and normal people, forgiveness injures narcissism—it hurts" (Vitz & Mango, 1997a, p. 74). "Forgiveness has the effect of destroying both the hated object (because one gives up the hate relationship) and the idealized object (which is recognized as being sullied, and needing forgiveness)" (Vitz & Mango, 1997b p. 70). The person's power relationship with the object-image is seriously threatened and permanently altered in unpredictable ways when one forgives, and the ego must relinquish control.

The choice of forgiveness and, in the instance of serious offense, the on-going process of forgiveness, can be a difficult choice to make and a wearying road to travel. It can be a desert experience. The case against it can be easily rationalized, the case for it can be hard to make. The mere suggestion of forgiving a person who has seriously wounded another can be viewed as threatening or self-injurious. However, wounding occurs in relationships, and it is through transforming a broken relationship *internally*, changing the image-representation of the offender, that healing can occur without risk of further injury.

The extant literature reveals that descriptions of forgiveness can be categorized as painful or difficult; therapeutic; set in the context of cognitive restructuring or in the context of object relations.

Descriptions that stress the difficulties include: Absorbing the pain (Bergin, 1988); the pain of intimacy (Hassel, 1985); an energy-depleting struggle (Enright, Gassin & Wu, 1992); a dying to desire for revenge (Hassel, 1985); a risky action

(Cunningham, 1985; Tihon, 1982); an act of embracing human fallibility (Halling, 1994); a struggle to release the violator while still feeling anger (Enright, Gassin & Wu, 1992); and recognition of serious injustice (Enright & Zell, 1989). These writers agree that forgiveness is "difficult and costly" (Worthington & DiBlasio, 1990, p. 223), and, it appears, the deeper the hurt, the higher the cost.

Why enter into a process of forgiving someone who has lost his or her right to receive such love (Enright, Gassin & Wu, 1992)? Descriptions that emphasize forgiveness as therapeutic in nature can help to answer this question. Forgiveness is also viewed as: an effective means of promoting personal and relational development (Ferch, 1998); that which brings relief and a sense of a new beginning in life (Halling, 1994); a therapeutic event of enormous power and importance (Ritzman, 1987); a profoundly transforming experience and central to the healing of one's brokenness (Bauer et al., 1992); that which frees the forgiving individual from the hard emotions of fear, anger, suspicion, mistrust, loneliness and alienation (Enright & Zell, 1989); and an internal, emotional release (Smedes, 1984). This movement or act of release is an inner response as opposed to reconciliation — a behavioral coming together (Enright & Zell, 1989) and as such poses no risk of further injury. The process is also viewed as humanizing, courageous, healthy and restorative (ibid).

Those descriptions set in the context of cognitive restructuring consider forgiveness to include releasing and giving up negative judgments about the offender (Enright, Gassin & Wu, 1992); a cognitive reframing (Cunningham, 1985); a choice made about how a person deals with the past (Hope, 1987); a willingness to pardon others (Gorsuch & Hao, 1993); a paradoxical act that releases a person through an upleveling or reframing process (Hope, 1987); and a choice between getting even or getting close (Simon & Simon, 1990).

Descriptions set in a context of object relations involve considering forgiveness as an aid in obtaining a higher level of object relations and object constancy (Vitz & Mango, 1997a); the integration of negative and positive object representations (Gartner, 1988); and a lengthy process of self- and object representations undergoing a series of re-modifications (Doyle,1999).

RETALIATION VS. CHOICE FOR CHANGE

Serious injury can be followed by anger and desire for revenge, which can then be projected in paranoid fashion onto the offender. This fear of retaliation, the end-result of the defense mechanism of projection, involves fear of reprisal, fear of the offender and fear of the offender-object. These emotions are directed at the object and rather than decathecting, the object ironically accumulates even more psychic energy. Not only is the goal of the wish-impulse thwarted—the opposite of the intended effect is produced. At this point the person can have cognitions such as "This is intolerable" or "This is inexcusable" or "I can't take any more of this." This "moment of refusal" is the antecedent for any scheme of revenge (Moss, 1986) whether such scheme has only internal expression, external expression, or both.

However, insult and injury, followed by hatred or desire for revenge, need not inevitably follow this path. Retaliation can be rejected at least as a behavioral possibility initially, by means of a *cognitive choice* involving enlightened self-interest, while the individual seeks to cope with the inevitable cognitions and emotions that are aroused. The person thereby transforms the "moment of refusal" into a moment of fertile opportunity. The goal is eventual decathexis of the object, or energy release, resulting in a peaceful inner state and freedom from both fear of reprisal and fear of loss of impulse control.

STAGES OF FORGIVENESS AND COGNITIVE RESTRUCTURING

Cognitive restructuring, involving an informed or enlightened choice can occur in the following manner, proceeding (over time) from the initial cognition to the restructured cognitive goal:

Initial Cognition	Cognitive Restructuring Goal
1. I'll get even.	1. I can't forgive him now; maybe later.
2. She's not worth the trouble.	2. I'll try to accept her human short-comings.
3. I can't stand his behavior.	3. I have needed to be forgiven and likely will again (recognition of human kinship).
4. I think I'll just ignore him.	4. Though I don't feel like forgiving, I *choose* to forgive him.
5. I'm not going to have anything to do with her.	5. I want to forgive her, but it's really hard.
6. His attitude really annoyed me.	6. I understand why he acted as he did and I'm ready to forgive him.
7. What she did really hurt and I'm very angry.	7. I release her from any debt owed to me. I do not hold her bound in any way.

If a person objects that forgiving re-victimizes him or her, it is important to recognize that it is not forgiveness but reconciliation that has such potential. It is when a person will not forgive that there can be revictimization by the on-going presence of internal turmoil and absence of inner peace.

It can be useful to view forgiveness as a process including gradated cognitions occurring over several stages, in various levels and with varying degrees of awareness. These stages include increasingly efficacious cognitions that are a part of each forgiveness stage. The following stages are identified:

I.   Preliminary: pre-forgiveness
II.   Transitional: conditional forgiveness
III. Readiness: cognitive choice of forgiveness
IV.   Forgiveness: repetition of choice and release
V.   Reconciliation: unconditional forgiveness combined with risk-taking behavior.

Descriptions of each state with corresponding cognitions follow.

I. Preliminary Stage

A person can be fully aware of the presence of hurt and anger following psychological injury, or fear can operate to produce avoidance of the re-experience of emotional pain. Denial or repression are the defense mechanisms used to preserve the integrity of the ego at this stage. There can be awareness of feelings such as hurt, anger, fear and guilt. A person can begin to acknowledge the depth of the hurt and that he or she has been violated. Anger might become strong or even consuming. Indignation can be present and there can be hatred and desire for revenge or at least justice. At this point the person could be considered to be in the preliminary stage. A person can be at varying levels of conscious awareness with regard to cognitions such as the following:

1. I will have revenge.
2. I plan to retaliate - I'll get even.
3. I want vengeance.
4. I refuse to accept an apology.
5. I cannot stand the person.
6. I must protect myself.

At this stage, the ego is primarily motivated to seek retaliation or revenge with possible concurrent fear of the violator. There is no cognitive choice by the ego for forgiveness. The inner state of the offended person can be that of bitterness.

II. Transitional Stage

Acknowledgment by the person of injury can bring self-blame, guilt, depression and confusion. There can be an experience of loss and a mourning process may ensue. There can also follow a new openness to the possibility of forgiveness. The cognitive choice to forgive can be made by the ego at this stage.

Cognitions, at varying levels of consciousness, can be such as the following:

7. I will not forgive unless I am vindicated.
8. I will not forgive unless I have justice.
9. I'll forgive if she apologizes.
10. I'll forgive if he promises not to hurt me again.
11. I'll forgive to get my heavenly reward.

Motivation is primarily (a) good of self, that is, the person becomes aware that forgiveness reduces chronic anger with its harmful physical and psychological effects or, (b) fear of divine retribution, e.g., the believing person might think, "I better do it because God says I should." There can be some choices made by the ego at this stage in the direction of forgiveness. The type of forgiveness is conditional. The inner state of the person could be described as bittersweet.

III. Readiness Stage

The person can achieve a degree of acceptance, that is, a partial integration of the offending event within his or her experience, by means of the effects of the aforementioned cognitive choice to forgive. There can subsequently follow an experience of inner release (Smedes, 1984) that involves an awareness of deeper forgiveness. The person can experience a new openness to the movement of grace at this stage. Emotions are beginning to "come on board," that is, to follow the ego's choice for forgiveness. Cognitions can be of the following type:

12. I choose to forgive.
13. I'm ready to forgive.
14. I'll accept his apology.
15. I'll pray for her good.
16. I'll ask God to help me forgive.
17. I'll forgive because I realize God has forgiven me.
18. I'm open to letting love de-sensitize me to the experience of offense.

Motivation at this level is (a) good of self; and (b) good of the offending individual. There are more cognitive choices made at this stage in the direction of forgiveness. It involves a fuller operation of God's grace and love. Forgiveness at this level is unconditional. The inner state of the client can be peaceful.

IV. Forgiveness Stage

At this level a person can be aware of a deeper experience of forgiveness than at earlier stages. However, with serious injury the person can experience a recurrence of anger. It would then be necessary for the ego to choose once again to forgive so that the process can continue to move forward. Such a dynamic can repeat numerous times depending on the degree or depth of psychological injury. Each occurrence can involve the re-emergence of anger, and necessitate a re-newed choice for forgiveness.

Cognitions can be as follows:

19. I forgive her again.
20. I don't hold him bound in any way.
21. There is no debt owed to me.
22. I release her.

Motivation is that of loving and attaining personal freedom. There is involvement of intellect, choice and feelings. It is further operation of God's grace in the life of the individual. Forgiveness at this stage is unconditional and fuller. The inner state of the person can be peaceful with a sense of new freedom because the offender, and the offender's inner image, no longer has the power to precipitate prolonged anger or resentment.

V. Reconciliation Stage

For those who so choose, a step toward the offender could take place at this stage. This can follow an awareness of new freedom present internally and restoration of peace in the relationship. The individual can experience him- or herself as stronger and aware of a new openness to relationship. There is awareness of risk involved, and a willingness to engage in risk-taking behavior. The person can place the offense in perspective and view it in the larger experiential context of the relationship. Cognitions can include the following:

23. I'm ready for a new beginning.
24. I'm willing to risk future hurt.
25. I prefer feelings of frustration, disappointment or sadness to feelings of anger, revenge, indignation or self-righteousness.

Motivation is for renewal and restoration or healing of the relationship. There can be movement in the relationship from discordance to concordance, and from disunity to a fuller union. The type of forgiveness is unconditional and full. The person's inner state can be that of harmonious peace and freedom. There is no power struggle at this point and a peaceful condition can prevail.

OBJECT FORMATION AND OBJECT RELATIONS

An object is an inexact and incomplete internal image-representation of a significant person in one's life. This image is perceived through a prism of needs, emotions and instincts such as sexual or aggressive impulses. (The term "introject" is perhaps more descriptive for some). This need-influenced image-representation is understood to be that which will satisfy the instinctive drive whether that drive is for unity with the object or for it's destruction. The object-image crystallizes around the memories, associations, feelings and thoughts associated with the significant individual. The image is a repository imbued with such mental contents and develops outside of conscious awareness.

Object relations include internalization of interpersonal relations that "contribute crucially to the development of the personality of the individual" (Kernberg, 1984, p. 59). In the instance of an experience of violation, negative emotions such as fear, anger or hate can play a role in the development of an object and impact ego development. Kernberg (1984, p. 76) states that "libidinally or aggressively determined affective states constitute the primary motive for internalization" of the relationships between self and others. Thoughts such as "I can't stand that person" or "I'll get even" reinforce the retention of hard emotions such as fear, anger and guilt. These thoughts and feelings are components in the construction of the object- representations and significantly influence the inner formation of the offender's image with potential for impact on subsequent ego development and interpersonal behavior.

An object forms in the dynamic unconscious from social relations with its human counterpart. Such images form to provide need-satisfaction, that is, to satisfy needs and impulses that are socially not sanctioned or are unacceptable to the individual. To illustrate: A man, much in need of retaining his present job and position, received a very poor performance evaluation from his supervisor. That very night he dreamed of being promoted beyond the supervisor's level such that his former supervisor now reported to him. In the dream, he exacted retribution (which may include retaliatory behavior disproportionate to the offense), that is, he took revenge on the object. Thus, a safe outlet was provided for discharge, or decathexis, of aggressive impulses, urges that could not otherwise be safely or easily expressed.

However, connective affect or instinctual drives related to an object need not be only of a negative nature. Feelings of love and affection can also find expression in object relations. For example, a woman worked in a maximum security setting for mentally-disordered patients with violent tendencies. As a social worker, part of her responsibilities included daily contact and provision of direct one-on-one psychological and social services. At times, security in this facility was not sufficient to protect her, in timely fashion, from a violent outburst by a patient. In time, she found herself dealing with a significant degree of anxiety and depression. As a single mother, she needed to continue in her job though she actively searched for another regularly, to no avail. The situation continued for years until such time as a social acquaintance offered her work of a much more positive, and safer, nature. She had a dream shortly after departing from her previous employment. In the dream, she passed through a doorway and found herself in what she described as "a place of great darkness." The dim surroundings were foreboding and fraught with unseen dangers. Twists and turns necessary to wend her way through the twilight haze seemed to place her in jeopardy of sudden and unpredictable attack. The feeling-tone of the dream was that of anxiety and bordered on panic. Nevertheless, she found that she was not alone in the dream, but was accompanied by a friend who seemed to possess a cognitive map of their surroundings. Arm in arm, the two made their way to a door that, once they passed through it, led them out of the place of darkness. On the other side, the two friends embraced, that is, the dreamer experienced and expressed profound love and gratitude to the object, the representational image of her social contact.

Kernberg (1984, pp. 33-34) explains: "…internalized object relations come to represent internally the external world as experienced by the developing ego. Actually, the enrichment of one's personal life by the internal presence of selective, partial identifications (objects and object constellations) representing people who are loved and admired in a realistic way…constitutes a major source of emotional depth and well-being." Objects and internal object relations can be an outlet for both socially acceptable and socially unacceptable drives.

EGO FORMATION AND FUNCTION

"(I)nternalized object relations constitute substructures of the ego…" (Kernberg, 1986, p. 5), that is, the ego takes form by means of a series of processes that internalize objects and object constellations. "Ego identity refers to the overall organization of …the world of objects" and is achieved by organizing such objects and object constellations into a coherent whole (Kernberg, 1984, p.32). Ego identity is also described as "a (refined) structuring of the internal world of (human-) objects…and refers to (organizing and integrating objects)…into a dynamic, unified structure" (Kernberg, 1984, pp. 32, 76). "(Such more or less permanent) object representations (nevertheless) experience *important modifications* (emphasis added) over the years under the influence of ego growth and later object relations" (Kernberg, 1984, p. 33). Though object relations constitute primarily an unconscious process, the resultant ego is capable of purposeful growth and development. At it's healthiest, the ego is a fluid, developing psychological structure that is comprised of both unconscious dynamics and increasing conscious awareness.

The ego, part conscious and part unconscious, is that part of the human psychè which categorizes, organizes, and synthesizes (human-) objects and object constellations, including self-objects, human-objects and connective affect. It is the "seat of consciousness, the (awareness) of oneself…as a person" (Kernberg, 1986, p. 228). The ego includes one's self-image and is a conceptualization of personal identity, of who I am and who I am not, "me" and "not-me," out of which flows intentional, purposeful behavior. The ego involves boundaries, attitudes, emotions, desires, passions, thoughts, perceptions and images.

The ego is reality-oriented and seeks to fulfill the person's wants and needs while acknowledging and responding to the legitimate needs of others. This reality orientation includes the person's need to love and receive love. At the same time, the ego, "is first and foremost, a body-ego," (Freud, 1923, p. 17) and seeks to preserve, defend and protect the body, and the psychè which resides in it. The experience of serious violation results in repulsion which, under the influence of aggressive fixation on the object, can result in disgust and hatred. The offender's internal image, whether conscious or unconscious, can cause distressing arousal and tension. Such arousal is experienced in the body, resulting in a state of disequilibrium. "We feel a repulsion from the object and hate it; this hate can then be intensified to the point of an aggressive tendency toward the object with the intention of destroying it" since "the ego hates, abhors, and pursues with intent to destroy all objects which are for it a source of painful feelings..." (Freud, 1915, pp. 100-101). With serious violation, the tension-producing, internalized image is experienced as a block to the instinct's (and the ego's) goal of satisfaction (Freud, 1915) and its destruction is regarded as that which will provide gratification.

With aggression directed at the object, an experience of temporary tension reduction reinforces the deceptive idea that the object has been defeated or destroyed. The ego deceptively experiences the goal, tension reduction through object destruction, as having been accomplished. With the eventual and inevitable return of tension, the ego again resorts to aggression and the process of aggressive fixation on the hated object is underway. Such fixation "puts an end to (the object's) mobility" (Freud, 1915, p. 88). The resulting "...repetition compulsion (is) largely a product of unchanged (and hated) internal images" (Doyle, 1999, p. 196). Yet, "...flexible internal images (can be critical) in fostering...life-long psychological growth" and "reconfigured internal representations (can play an important role) in unraveling the strange-hold repetition compulsion can have on optimal human development" (Doyle, 1999, pp. 195, 196).

In contrast, when the ego makes an informed choice of forgiveness, fixation on the enemy-object can *begin* to diminish. The choice of forgiveness disrupts the repetitive, instinctual attachment to the object and initiates a process whereby the object, "the most variable thing about an instinct..." (Freud, 1915, p. 87) can begin to change form from hated and tension-producing to innocuous and tension-reducing. The image representing the violator, when forgiven, no longer has the power to arouse tension-inducing bodily states. The choice of forgiveness signals the beginning of the end of the repetitive cycle of object-directed anger and discharge, attained through the more permanent decathectic properties of the forgiveness process. Such a choice is a true gift to self, as well, since fixation involving repetitive "impulses of aggression against the object (which seek) to destroy the object...(are followed by) a systematic torturing of the object and interminable *self-torment*...(emphasis added) (Freud, 1923, pp. 43-44), since the object-image exists as an internalized part of the human psychè. Aggressive impulses repetitively directly at the object result in anxiety and, quite likely, guilt when a formerly loved object is involved. Under such conditions, there can only be inner conflict and tension, a self-punishing effect.

The ego, conscious and unconscious, functions as a mediator between the self and the person's world of relationships. On a conscious level, the ego thinks and reasons, seeks to employ communication effectively to resolve conflicts that arise in relationships, and seeks to obtain personal and relational satisfaction. It is involved in reality testing and adaptation to reality, and yet is capable of serious self-deception. On a generally unconscious level, it is that part of the human psychè that uses defense mechanisms to reduce anxiety and bolster self-esteem. The ego can be rigid and unbending, or fluid and dynamic. The ego negotiates and compromises, tolerates ambiguity, and can be flexible. The ego seeks to defend the person's sense of well-being and to reduce tension and/or anxiety, which are experienced as occurring in the body.

One function of the ego is to obtain satisfaction for need states, getting one's needs met in relationships, while at the same time growing in the capacity to love others and participate in loving, fulfilling relations. To love and be loved is proffered as a prime function and goal of the healthy ego. Offenses and conflicts with significant others potentially frustrate the accomplishment of this goal. With the experience of serious violation, the ego's relationship to a formerly loved object is transformed in the direction of hating the object, resulting in an alteration of the ego, which has a weakening effect. "(D)epression, despair, irritability, impatience, tension and cynicism" (Vitz and Mango, 1997a, p. 78), resulting from such hatred "used as a pathological defense" can only reduce the ego's capacity for effective conflict resolution. With hatred, the ability to use anger constructively is markedly impaired or obstructed by increased potential for "destructive acting-out…violence, passive-aggression (or) apathetic withdrawal…:" (ibid), the latter an expression of love's opposite, indifference. With such hatred there can also be present "fear of retaliation due to unconscious, violent impulses" (ibid), paranoid anxiety (Hunter, 1978) and fear of loss of impulse control, all of which weaken the ego's ability to function effectively.

The solution revolves around a fluidity being restored to immobilized objects, resulting in a developing, healthy ego that is not tied to unchanging forms and images. It is important for the ego to be flexible and adaptive. But violation can make a person rigid, hypervigilant, anxious and reactive rather than proactive and spontaneously responsive. Forgiveness restores mutability to the object and, by extension, adaptability to the ego. Such fluid ego function includes an openness to change, an openness to object transformation. Doyle (1999, abstract) describes forgiveness as exactly that—"a lengthy process of self- and object representations...undergoing a series of re-modifications." Forgiveness eventually accomplishes positive, healthy object transformation by decathecting offensive internal images and depriving them of their proclivity for producing on-going tension and anxiety.

Contempt and hatred of the offending object constitute the negative affect that can powerfully connect the ego to the image. Such "connecting negative affect" results in a "bad self-representation" (Gartner, 1988, p. 316), that is, the person's self-image and sense of self-worth are negatively affected. Even when the ego has such negative connection with the object by reason of aggressive impulses directed at it, reconciliation *internally* with the offending image-representation poses no real threat. Actually, "unity, or tendency toward unity...is particularly characteristic of the ego" (Freud, 1923, p. 35) and the ego's aim, through forgiveness, is for "union...reconciliation" (Moss, 1986, p. 208). Hatred places the ego in internal conflict and interferes with the ego's unitive goal. Internal integrity and inner peace suffer; growth is stunted through aggressive fixation rendering the object immutable.

The moment before forgiveness is a moment of danger and opportunity, a time of futility and potential fertility. The danger involves entering into obsession, the repetitive thinking and re-thinking about the violating event. The embodied ego seeks retribution as a means of restoring homeostasis and psychological balance. Revenge appears as a sweet solution, a remedy to the experience of "excess" (Moss, 1986, p. 205). There is a bitterness in the psychè and a "moment of refusal" which is viewed as "the prelude for any scheme of revenge" (Moss, 1986, p. 198).

In contrast to a scheme of revenge, there can instead be a strategy of forgiveness. The choice of forgiveness means openness to new internalized forms uninhibited and unhindered by the violation of the past, free to continue unimpeded in the healing and growing processes (Fittipaldi, 1982). Forgiveness transforms the object(s), building blocks of the ego and ego identity, re-directing the ego toward health and growth. By means of the forgiveness process, transformed objects result in a transformed and strengthened ego. A threatening object can become benign if not actually amiable. An object will not permanently disappear, but it can be made less threatening. The image, after forgiveness, is neither hated nor feared. The transformed object no longer creates a tension or anxiety within. It is decathected and devoid of negative affect. The cycle of the repetition compulsion involving hate, retaliation and (self-) punishment is ended. There are numerous hidden and ultimately positive, strengthening effects when a person chooses to enter into the forgiveness process.

BEYOND THE WOUNDED EGO

After the conscious choice to forgive is made, a process is set in motion which is both dynamic and mysterious. Even if God is not consciously acknowledged and intentionally sought, humans need a forgiving Other to bridge the real gap between the ego's capability (or incapability) and the realization of forgiveness (Gartner, 1988; Ashbrook, 1988; Moss, 1986). For those of the Christian faith, that mediator who stands in the gap is Jesus (John 16:23, 24; Acts 4:12; 1 Tim. 2:5,6). Obviously, people of all faiths or those with no particular religious beliefs can forgive. The Lord of life aids those who choose forgiveness during life's journey, whether or not they acknowledge Him as their source of empowerment.

The choice for forgiveness sets up a classic and on-going struggle within: "For what our human nature wants is opposed to what the Spirit wants and what the Spirit wants is opposed to what our human nature wants...it is precisely because the two are so opposed that you do not always carry out your good intentions" (Gal. 15:17-18; TEV, JB). Further, "I fail to carry out the things I want to do, and I find myself doing the very things I hate...though the will to do what is good is in me, the performance is not..." (Rom. 7:15-16, 18; JB). It is a struggle common to humanity (1 Cor. 10:13; NIV). Though neither faith nor recourse to God are necessary to choose forgiveness, the victory is ultimately achieved by God's life working in and through human processes (Nee, 1998).

STRUGGLE AND INNER RECONCILATION

Even after the process of forgiveness is well under way, a thought, association, image or memory can cause the hard emotion of anger to act like a thick rubber band stretched to its limit, pulling the person back suddenly to the feared and/or hated object. The object is not yet totally transformed and the aggressive impulse seeks discharge to reduce the inner state of tension.

When the person can instead offer a prayer of forgiveness for the offender and stand in his or her place, Imitatio Dei (in imitation of God), the person can initiate a grace-filled action. The one violated comes before God in the place of the one who committed the offense. This substitutionary reparation imitates Christ who, in Christian belief, took onto Himself the offenses of anyone who would accept His act of atonement. It is perhaps unusual to be willing to "pay" for someone else's offense, and perhaps more unusual still when that offense has been experienced by oneself. However, such an act can help to make the paradox a reality: loss becomes gain.

The individual absorbs the pain, accepting the loss, in return for this gain. For those who choose to forgive, the rewards include freedom enhanced, peace restored, life renewed. Forgiveness is admittedly costly but the results of the informed ego's choice to forgive can be far-reaching. It is a powerful force for physical, psychological, and spiritual healing.

Choosing to forgive ultimately brings about inner reconciliation with the object and with God who is light (1 John 1: 5, JB). Moss describes forgiveness as a process of going "through" the formerly hated object to the Creator who is "radiance," i.e., the light of the world (Moss, 1986, p. 208; John 9:5, 12:46; RSV). The offender, a human being nevertheless, is made in the image of God (Gen. 1:26; James 3:9; JB). His or her object can be re-imaged as such when brought into the light of God's love and forgiveness.

CLINICAL ILLUSTRATION AND APPLICATION

When there is openness to forgiveness, a person can proceed through the following steps:

1. The individual makes the initial choice to forgive. There will not likely be any immediate relief from negative emotions such as anger, distrust, rejection or a sense of betrayal.
2. A person can be aided in his or her understanding of objects by means of an association with dream images. Object relations "may be considered a crossroad where instinct (e.g., aggression) and the social system meet..." (Kernberg, 1984, p. 59) and can be diagrammed as in Figure 1.
3. The choice of cognitions that include releasing the offender (relinquishing) and refusing to lay claim to any debt owed (not seeking redress) will begin to result in decreased anger and tension.
4. With serious offense, return of some negative emotion is to be expected and it is important to re-choose forgiveness at such times. The forgiveness process and its duration is not under the conscious control of the ego and roughly corresponds to the degree or depth of hurt and offense. Also, duration partially depends on the person's previous experience with forgiving and inward propensity for or against the

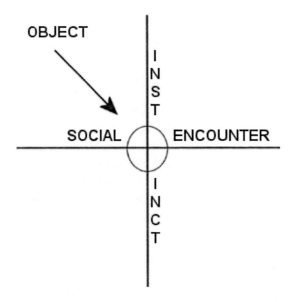

Figure 1. Interaction of Instinct and Social Relations Leading to Object Formation

process. Ultimately, after the choice is made, the time at which the forgiveness process is completed rests with a Power beyond human control.

5. Forgiveness aids the person in obtaining a higher level of object relations that have a freeing and peace-inducing effect (Vitz & Mango, 1997a). One result of genuine forgiveness is that "a person's object relations are healthier" (ibid, p. 77). Evidence includes increased "ability to use anger constructively" and "a general increase in affects such as peace, joy and hope…" (ibid, p. 78).

The following is a clinical illustration of applied object relations in the treatment of serious injury with potential for chronic anger and hatred: A husband who was neglectful and rejecting of his wife learned that she was having an affair. When he confronted his wife, she agreed to end the relationship. The husband, trying to process the painful feelings and offense, pressed the wife for information such as, times, places and other details. The wife provided this information, hoping to satisfy her husband and perhaps alleviate her guilt. However, this knowledge resulted in the husband's experience of further anger. The wife, in guilty fashion, would then try to appease her husband by providing more information about the affair and the other man when her husband requested it. This only served to re-fuel his hurt and anger, and the cycle would repeat.

Applying the above five-step procedure to this clinical example, the person makes the choice to forgive (Step 1) and the husband shifts his focus from the persons involved to his inner experience of them, that is, their hidden images. Dream interpretation can be quite useful at this point. Objects and object relations are understood as at (Step 2) and the husband begins relinquishing thoughts of anger or retaliation (Step 3). He stops pressing his wife for details about the affair. This can only result in further hurtful emotions and angry thoughts that are counter-productive. Such thoughts and feelings will return (Step 4), probably a number of times, and it is important to re-choose forgiveness at those times. The husband releases those thoughts and feelings through forgiveness rather than re-hash them with his wife or use them to retaliate. Step 5 can be attained after choosing and re-choosing to forgive with intermittent periods that include release of negative affect. At other times anger can return, though increasingly diminished.

An incident such as the affair described in this clinical example will not likely be forgotten. "When one forgives, he or she rarely forgets the event. People tend to recall traumatic events, but on forgiving, a person may remember in new ways..." (Baskin & Enright, 2004, p. 80). Though not forgotten, the offense can be forgiven, and forgiveness will take the sting out of the psychological wound.

CONCLUSION

Hatred, as a pathological defense, can only prolong the misery that accompanies tension, anxiety and, quite likely, obsessive thought and/or depression associated with fixation on unforgiven (human-) objects. Hatred can feel safe and powerful. However, the psychological cost and energy required to maintain it can be sustained for a finite time only. Satisfaction through hatred or revenge is temporary, fleeting, and, ultimately, self-destructive. A Chinese proverb states, "When you seek revenge, dig two graves." Allowed to persist unchecked, anger, initially benign, can harden into hatred with its serious harmful personal and relational effects. Hate, while at times a pathological defense, is also a choice. Hatred, unlike anger, "is not an immediate reaction, but rather depends upon the cultivation of anger. The injunction not to let the sun go down on one's anger is presumably aimed at preventing the development of hatred and the serious problems that usually go with it. (A)dults…either freely decide to accept their hatred or to work at rejecting it. (H)atred in most adults at its core is not affect but volition" (Vitz & Mango, 1997 b, pp. 65, 68). Immediately after the onset of anger, there is an important choice to be made. That choice has far-reaching consequences for the individual's health, well-being and relationships.

Cognitive restructuring and object transformation, as integral parts of the forgiveness process, have the following mental, emotional and relational benefits in common with forgiveness: 1) all promote release of the painful violation, 2) all can help produce positive change in significant relationships, 3) all contribute to healing of painful memories, 4) all help to reduce tension and anxiety, 5) all can eventually result in catharsis or emotional release, 6) all can free up previously blocked mental and emotional energy, 7) all promote or restore psychological and spiritual harmony in relationship with one's Creator and, 8) in addition to psychological wellness, all can promote physical health as well (Kaplan, 1992; Miller et al., 1996; Thoresen et al., 1998).

Forgiveness has specific application as a therapeutic procedure for certain challenging issues and disorders. Baskin and Enright (2004, p. 89) point out that "(T)here are certain emotional health issues for which forgiveness counseling is particularly well-suited, such as incest survivors, adolescents hurt by emotionally distant parents, and men hurt by the abortion decision of a partner." Further, chronic anger can be considered as an etiological factor for some clients with "conduct disorder, oppositional defiant disorder, mood disorders and anxiety disorders" (ibid). Also, "a number of mental health issues are significantly related to anger such as sexual abuse, divorce and family-of-origin concerns" (ibid, p. 88). Worthington and DiBlasio (1990) propose a practical and effective forgiveness regimen for processing hurt and anger in the marriage relationship. For anger-based disorders or anger that is a mask for fear, the efficacy of forgiveness as a therapeutic intervention is being increasingly demonstrated.

The challenge of forgiveness, as a healthy alternative to hatred, includes coming face-to-face with some limitations in human psychological make-up. A person cannot complete the forgiveness process by his or her own power. Though necessary, cognitive choice is insufficient to bring about forgiveness (Baskin & Enright, 2004). Object transformation is beyond the person's control or ability to directly accomplish. Powerful feelings set in motion following serious violation typically lead not to forgiveness but to desire for revenge, aggressive behavior, or guilt and depression when anger is turned inward.

However, forgiveness is not bound by human limitations. Forgiveness, as "a nodal point at the interface of psychotherapy and religion" (Hope, 1987, p. 240), is a process that has an inexhaustible Source of empowerment. By being receptive to the forgiveness process, human beings are empowered to offer the healing gift to self and others.

REFERENCES

Ashbrook, J. B. (Eds.) (1988). *Paul Tillich in conversation*. Bristol, IN: Wyndham Hall Press.

Baskin, T. W. & Enright, R. D. (2004). Intervention studies on forgiveness: A meta-analysis. *Journal of Counseling and Development, 82*, 79-90.

Bauer, L., Duffy, J., Fountain, E., Halling, S., Holzer, M., Jone, E., Leifer, M. & Rowe, J. O. (1992). Exploring self-forgiveness. *Journal of Religion and Health, 31*, 149-160.

Bergin, A. E. (1988). Three contributions of a spiritual perspective to counseling, psychotherapy and behavior change. *Counseling and Values, 33*, 21-30.

Cunningham, B. B. (1985). The will to forgive: A pastoral theological view of forgiving. *The Journal of Pastoral Care, 39*, 141-149.

Doyle, G. (1999). Forgiveness as an intrapsychic process. *Psychotherapy, 36*, 190-198.

Enright, R. D. & Zell, R. L. (1989). Problems encountered when we forgive one another. *Journal of Psychology and Christianity, 8*, 52-60.

Enright, R. D., Gassin, E. A. & Wu, C. R. (1992). Forgiveness: A developmental view. *Journal of Moral Education, 21*, 99-114.

Ferch, S. R. (1998). Intentional forgiving as a counseling intervention. *Journal of Counseling and Development, 76*, 261-269.

Fittipaldi, S. E. (1982). Zen-Mind, Christian Mind, Empty Mind. *Journal of Ecumenical Studies, 19*, 69-84.

Freud, S. (1915). Instincts and their vicissitudes. *General psychological theory*. New York: Collier Books.

Freud, S. (1923). *The ego and the id*. New York: W. W. Norton.

Gartner, J. (1988). The capacity to forgive: An object relations perspective. *Journal of Religion and Health, 27*, 313-320.

Good News Bible: Today's English Version (TEV) (1976). New York: American Bible Society.

Gorsuch, R. L. & Hao, J. Y. (1993). Forgiveness: An exploratory factor analysis and its relationships to religious variables. *Review of Religious Research, 34*, 333-347.

Halling, S. (1994). Embracing human fallibility: On forgiving oneself and forgiving others. *Journal of Religion and Health*, *33*, 107-113.

Hassel, D. J. (1985). Prayer of forgiveness: The pain of intimacy. *Review for Religious*, May-June, 388-397.

Holy Bible, New International Version (NIV) (1978). Grand Rapids, MI: Zondervan Bible Publishers.

Hope, D. (1987). The healing paradox of forgiveness. *Psychotherapy 24*, 240-244.

Hunter, R. C. A. (1978). Forgiveness, retaliation and paranoid reactions. *Canadian Psychiatric Association Journal, 23,* 167-173.

Jerusalem Bible (JB) (1966). Garden City, N.Y.: Doubleday.

Kaplan, B. H. (1992). Social health and the forgiving heart: The type B story. *Behavioral Medicine, 15,* 3-14.

Kernberg, O. F. (1984). *Object relations theory and clinical psychoanalysis.* Northvale, N. J.: Jason Aronson, Inc.

Kernberg, O. F. (1986). Severe Personality Disorders. New Haven: Yale University Press

Miller, T. Q., Smith, T. W., Turner, C. W., Guijarro, M. L. & Hallet, A. (1996). A meta-analytic review of research on hostility and physical health. *Psychological Bulletin, 119*, 322-348.

Moss, D. B. (1986). Revenge and forgiveness. *American Imago*, *43*, 191-210.

Nee, W. (1998). *The spiritual man, Volumes 1, 2, and 3.* Anaheim, CA: Living Stream Ministry.

Pingleton, J. P. (1997). Why we don't forgive: A Biblical and object relations theoretical model for understanding failures in the forgiveness process. *Journal of Psychology and Theology*, *25*, 403-413.

Ritzman, T. A. (1987). Forgiveness: its role in therapy. *Medical Hypnoanalysis Journal*, *2*, 4-13.

Revised Standard Version Interlinear Greek-English New Testament (RSV) (1958). Grand Rapids, MI: Zondervan Publishing House.

Simon, S. & Simon S. (1990). *Forgiveness: How to make peace with your past and get on with your life.* New York: Warner.

Smedes, L. B. (1984). *Forgive and forget.* San Francisco: Harper & Row.

Thoresen, C. E., Luskin, F. & Harris, A. H. S. (1998). The science of forgiving interventions: Reflections and suggestions. In E. L. Worthington, Jr. (Eds.) *Dimensions of forgiveness* (163-190). Radnor, PA: Templeton Foundation Press.

Tihon, P. (1982). On the right moment for reconciliation. *Lumen Vitae, 37*, 183-190.

Vitz, P. C. & Mango, P. (1997a). Kernbergian dynamics and religious aspects of the forgiveness process. *Journal of Psychology and Theology*, *25*, 72-80.

Vitz, P. C. & Mango, P. (1997b). Kleinian psychodynamics and religious aspects of hatred as a defense mechanism. *Journal of Psychology and Theology*, *25*, 64-71.

Worthington, E. L. & DiBlasio, F. A. (1990). Promoting mutual forgiveness within the fractured relationship. *Psychotherapy*, *27*, 219-223.

In: Psychology of Hate   ISBN: 978-1-61668-050-3
Editors: Carol T. Lockhardt, pp.83-101   © 2010 Nova Science Publishers, Inc.

Chapter 4

DO YOU HATE ME? HAVE I HURT YOU?: DEFENSES AGAINST GROWTH, SEPARATION, AND INDIVIDUATION THAT CREATE INTERPRETIVE ENACTMENTS PART ONE: FENDER BENDERS AND THE SHARED DEFENSIVE SYSTEMS OF LESS DIFFICULT PATIENTS

Robert Waska[*]
Institute for Psychoanalytic Studies,
Private Psychoanalytic Practice in San Francisco
and Marin County, CA, USA

ABSTRACT

All patients struggle with psychological conflicts regarding love, hate, and knowledge. Some patients are troubled by phantasies of causing hurt and hatred in the object as a result of their quest for separation, individuation, and personal creativity. Success, ambition, differentiation, growth, change, and

[*] Corresponding author: E-mail: drwaska@aol.com, Telephone: 415-883-4235, P.O. Box 2769 San Anselmo, CA 94979 USA

personal difference are all seen as creating, injury, unhappiness, anger, hatred, and rejection in the object. Therefore, these patients create intense and rigid defensive patterns of submissive, subordinate, and passive relating to prevent these internal catastrophes. These defensive mechanisms are mobilized through projective identification and create frequent patterns of interpretive enactments and counter-transference acting out.

This paper will highlight these vexing and humbling patterns of interpretive acting out we often find ourselves in as we try to reach out to patients but barely find a foothold before they slip away or before we lose our own therapeutic balance. Case material will be used for illustration to specifically examine how the defensive avoidance of certain wishes, feelings, and secret needs become part of the counter-transference and influence or pervert the interpretive process. As a result, the analyst may indeed be making helpful and accurate interpretations while also missing out on the more core aspects of the patient's in the moment phantasy and internal conflict. Theoretical and clinical material will be used to examine this phenomenon.

INTRODUCTION

From a Kleinian perspective, all patients struggle with psychological desires and conflicts regarding love, hate, and knowledge. Some patients are troubled by phantasies of causing hurt and hatred in the object as a result of their quest for separation, individuation, and personal creativity. Success, ambition, differentiation, growth, change, and personal difference are all seen as creating, injury, unhappiness, anger, hatred, and rejection in the object. Therefore, these patients create intense and rigid defensive patterns of submissive, subordinate, and passive relating to prevent these internal catastrophes. These defensive mechanisms are mobilized through projective identification and create frequent patterns of interpretive enactments and counter-transference acting out.

This chapter will highlight these vexing and humbling patterns of interpretive acting out we often find ourselves in as we try to reach out to patients but barely find a foothold before they slip away or before we lose our own therapeutic balance. Case material will be used for illustration to specifically examine how the defensive avoidance of certain wishes, feelings, and secret needs become part of the counter-transference and influence or pervert the interpretive process. As a result, the analyst may indeed be making helpful and accurate interpretations while also missing out on the more core aspects of the patient's in the moment phantasy and internal conflict. Theoretical and clinical material will be used to examine this phenomenon.

Patients come to us with very complex and troubling emotional struggles and we do our best to assist them in untying the mental knots and understanding how they may be continuing to tie themselves up. However, along the way in helping them learn and change, it is common if not predictable and unavoidable, that we face failure in our efforts. We come to find a wide spectrum of destructiveness in our patient's internal world yet we step in to help them learn about it and find resolve and integration. We encounter difficult moments at every turn and often have to pick up the pieces as we go. Counter-transference and projective identification are always found in conjunction with the transference and therefore make for sticky and chaotic clinical situations that can cause various forms of acting out between both parties but also can lead to a new clarity and internal shift.

It is common to be nudged, seduced or invited in subtle unconscious and interpersonal ways to be the spokesperson for the patient's unwanted aggressive, erotic, competitive, or defiant feelings and phantasies. In this forms of enactments, the analyst ends up making interpretations that basically voice the unwanted or sinful experiences for the patient, taking him or her out of the spotlight and taking on the risk or shame. This occurs through projective identification and counter-transference cycles that produce patterns of acting out or enactments by the analyst. So, a patient who is scared of being put in his place by the phantasy of a strict father might describe a situation in which he wanted to leave work to go play a game of basketball with his buddies, but he would describe it as a situation in which he felt he "probably should stay late at work because after all, lots of people are depending on him for this important project". The analyst would be, through projective identification and counter-transference patterns, become the holder and now spokesperson for the patient's defiant and guilty wishes. So, the interpretive enactment might be that the analyst says, "You really wanted to toss work to the side and head out to the courts. It was time for fun! But, you feel guilty about it". Here, the interpretation would be correct, but the patient has projected his guilty phantasy into the analyst and has the analyst voice this indulgence for him, thus avoiding the risk and not having to take responsibility for it. Due to projective identification and counter-transference, the excitement and defiance resides in the analyst not the patient.

Often in our best attempts at interpretation, we end up still emphasizing one side of things and neglecting other sides. This is unavoidable since there are always many facets to the patient's conflicts. However, the patient may be inviting us or pushing us in one direction or another and through our own counter-transference wishes or fears, we may side with the patient's defensive strategies and end up interpreting one aspect of their phantasies over another.

As I mentioned in the short example, we often end up interpreting the conflicts our patients have because we have been tricked into being the voice for their id impulses and they then avoid their potential superego punishment. In other situations, our own counter-transference of defiance, rebelliousness, or empathy for the underdog pulls us into making interpretations that are basically routing the patient on to do what he or she wants to but feels some superego judgment about. I believe this is the more common mistake that we interpretively make and the easier one to notice as the combination of projective identification and counter-transference is a fairly predictable and obvious one to eventually notice.

INTERPRETIVE ENACTMENTS AND THE PROJECTIVE DEFENSES AGAINST DIFFERENTIATION

In this paper, I will use case material to show the more difficult to notice interpretive enactments that occur with patients who use projective identification and how our counter-transference can be clouded to over interpret the shy, weak, or in need of protection side of the patient's phantasy and we end up ignoring, denying, or minimizing the more aggressive, independent, and separate aspects of their phantasies and feelings. Since these feelings tend to be saturated with guilt, anxiety, fear, and ownership of these desires is felt to be toxic or dangerous to both self and object. So, the patient unconsciously wants and hates their own independent desires, struggling to promote their own ambitions and hopes as wells as attacking them at the same time. Therefore, when counter-transference is colored by projective identification of these intense conflicts, the analyst can have a blind spot to these phantasies because he wants to protect the patient from that self judgment and hate or wants to avoid conflict with the punitive object.

These clinical moments in which we slip and fall into a variety of enactments with our patients are not fatal to the treatment but cause momentary friction or detour in the analytic process. The contemporary Kleinian approach embraces the clinical idea that projective identification and counter-transference often combine in unavoidable ways to nudge the analyst to subtly or strongly act out certain object relational phantasies with the patient. Previously (Waska 2006), I have written about how the interpretive process is a frequent stage for these moments in which we make interpretations that are both correct and helpful but also an aspect of counter-transference guilt, hostility, collusion, desire, or defense.

Specifically, I have noted in other publications how often one side of the patient's conflict is acted out by the analyst. Often, it is the role of guide, permissive parent, soothing caretaker, or encouraging coach for the illicit, censored, unwanted, or prohibited feelings and thoughts the patient struggles with. So, the analyst ends up doing the dirty work and interprets the very thing the patient wishes to say or do but doesn't want to risk. Therefore, I have previously examined this hidden, projected side of the patient's phantasy. In this paper, however, I will outline a similar situation, but one that has more to do with the patient's projection of core defensive judgments and decries than the projection of raw impulses or rebellious protest. The case material will show the analyst's temporary collusion with the patient' defensive structure and self-hatred of change, differentiation, or growth.

Case Material

Interpretive slips or clinical "fender benders" are often temporary, but sometimes ongoing, moments that are unnoticed or denied by the analyst in which the patient's pathological organization (Rosenfeld 1971 Steiner 1987) or psychic retreat (Steiner 1993) is shared by the analyst. My patient David had spoken many times over his two year analysis of feeling "stranded on Mount Everest without a jacket". This phantasy would come up whenever he revealed hidden wishes, forbidden anger, or strong desires to be different rather than pleasing or conforming to the object.

So, in the transference, he imagined I would be disapproving if he wanted to go fishing on the weekend instead of staying at home with his family or if he asked me to change our meeting time so he could go to the gym during his lunch break. When David revealed these sorts of forbidden feelings and censored thoughts to me, he felt extremely exposed and vulnerable. Hence, he associated to being stuck on Mount Everest without a jacket, facing the icy winds alone on this desolate peak. For the first year of treatment, I interpreted this image as him risking showing me a more masculine, striving side of himself but then feeling scared and alone, against the icy wind of my possible judgment and rejection. This was based on counter-transference feelings and a counter-transference impression of him as a vulnerable little boy, passive and hoping for my aid and care. Now, I believe this was and is true and that my interpretations of his phantasy was helpful in exploring this scared little boy flexing his new muscles but unsure of how father would respond. He wondered whether I would encourage him or disapprove and would I love him or hate him for having his own identity. David wanted my protection and encouragement as well as my reassurance that it was not bad or dangerous to be himself. He wanted to know that I wouldn't leave him there to freeze to death on the mountain top for his sins.

But, I eventually realized I had been in collusion with David on another level. There had been a fender bender. While I think I was accurate and helpful in pursuing the fear and punishment angle of his exposing a more strong, personal, and opinionated side of himself, I had been missing another side of his conflicts and phantasies. Both of us had focused on the scary and submissive side of being on Mount Everest without protection and we had avoided or hidden the more dominate, exhibitionistic, and proud aspect of the phantasy.

So, during one session he was telling me about going fishing on the weekend and catching "several decent size trout!" Then, he expressed how guilty and worried he was about the fallout from his family. I mentioned he might also worry about my opinion and would I be proud of his big catch or upset that he wasn't a responsible family man. He said, "Yes. After I tell you about it, I feel I am up there on a ledge, on Mount Everest without a jacket fighting the elements with the snow in my face". At that point, I reflected on my own counter-transference associations of what he was describing. I pictured a masculine mountain climber boldly conquering Mount Everest with a bare chest and success in his eyes. This image, a counter-transference phantasy formed by what my patient was not saying but possibly feeling and then needing to eject through projective identification, helped me realize there was more to the picture than just his fear and guilt. There was also hidden pride, aggression, and virility. So, I also noticed how we had both participated in this cloaked secret, only illuminating one side of his personality.

Now, I was able to make more balanced interpretations. I said, "I think you want to emphasize the scared and guilty feelings and hide the side of you that has conquered the mountain. After all, you are on top of the tallest and most difficult mountain in the world, single handedly making it to the top. You feel like a strong successful man, but are trying to hide that from me". David paused and then said, "I haven't ever thought of it that way. But, I see what you mean. I think that is right. I do feel like a real success some times and I want to wear that. But, I am not sure you want that or will allow it".

So, after a prolonged interpretive impasse or what I call a therapeutic fender bender, we were now able to work on a new and much more important aspect of David's phantasy life and his inner conflicts. This was not an instant transformation in the treatment but it did begin a very successful period in which he began to work through his anxieties around being competitive, equal, different, and opinionated. He hated this side of himself less and less. David was more able to work on how and why he needed to camouflage his pride and desire with masochistic submission and guilt. We were more in touch with how he liked to flex his muscles rather than how he felt punished for flexing them. He was gradually more able to work with my interpretations regarding how he hid his more phallic side by controlling me with this more needy, exposed image of a helpless junior climber in need of a jacket. I said, "You don't think I can handle you being a man, as if I will be shown up as weak or you will feel like we are in competition. You don't like to have us be two men hanging out together".

With this gradual shift in my interpretive direction, we were more able to better address the wider view of David's internal world. This therapeutic fender bender had caused some minor damage or delay to the analytic procedure but now we were more involved in an integrative process and were better able to maintain analytic contact (Waska 2007) in a creative and healing manner.

DISCUSSION

Betty Joseph (1988) has suggested that object relations theory should be constantly rediscovered and refreshed within the clinical situation by analysts focusing on not just what is being communicated by words but by what is being lived out in the transference. I would extend this idea to include an ongoing focus on what is being lived out in the counter-transference and in the interpretive process. This has much to do with the nature of the projective identification climate within the analytic situation and how those projections make up the core transference phantasies. As Joseph (1988) has noted, these projections can stimulate and provoke the analyst to act out the patient's phantasy life. I believe this often occurs through the interpretive field in which the analyst ends up making interpretations in either a defensive or anti-defensive mode, based on what elements are being projected.

In this paper, the case material illustrates interpretive enactments in which the patient's defensive stance was embedded within the interpretation, thus temporarily acting out the projective identification dynamic. Hinshelwood (1989) explains how the analyst, when being projected into, will respond with one of two counter-transference feelings. Either he will experience the anger, guilt, excitement, or whatever the patient is projecting or he will experience the patient's defenses against them, such as denial, manic triumph, guilt, anxiety, and so forth. Brenman (1985) has also noted a similar idea. He describes how patients are fairly attuned to the analyst's mind and tend to selectively project into certain aspects of the analyst's mind, including the analyst's defensive system. The clinical material will continue to show how this occurs within the purview of the analyst's interpretive function, distorting and deadening the analyst's ability to interpret in a whole object manner and instead selectively interpreting in a manner that colludes with the patient's own defenses against certain dangerous feelings and phantasies.

Case Material

The patient's projective identification dynamics can coerce the analyst to act out, via interpretation, various roles in the patient's unconscious phantasy life. Counter-transference sensitivities may increase the chance of this occurring. This interpretive acting out may be subtle and passive or more aggressive and active. If not monitored, contained, and understood, it can be destructive to the therapeutic envelope. We can become seductive, persecutory, guilt-inducing, or withdrawing by noting one aspect of the patient's internal issues in our interpretations and not another. When interpretively acting out, the analyst may end up participating actively or passively within these pathological cycles. All these types of acting out are inevitable but must be constantly monitored and worked through with the aid of the counter-transference.

If properly handled, these therapeutic fender benders can shed important light on otherwise hidden aspects of the patient's internal struggles and conflicts that are up to that moment only accessible through a projective identification process. While these moments of interpretive acting out can coincide with uncorrupted interpretive work, the overall analytic contact (Waska 2007) can suffer. While such acting out is probably unavoidable, the quicker the analyst can notice, contain, and understand such deviations, the better chance analytic contact can be reestablished and maintained.

Sarah was raised with her two sisters by parents who were very strict and critical. Sarah's father was particularly demanding in that he constantly told Sarah what she should be doing with her life and always added how she was failing his expectations. She loved him and felt they had some degree of resolution in their relationship before he died five years ago, but she still views her parents as "never really understanding her and quick to find fault. It was hard for them to ever imagine what I might be going through, whether it is positive or negative".

During her career as a hospital manager, Sarah was frequently told she was too slow and disorganized. Part of this was the result of her emotional struggle with authority, in particular with men, and feeling the need to take on everything so she could please the authority she also resented. But, taking on everything meant she was always overwhelmed and did a sloppy job as a result, displeasing her bosses. At the same time, she always felt very fatigued. During a routine physical examination, it turned out she had a neurological disease which would only get worse over time. She went out on disability about the same time she began her psychoanalysis.

Now in her fourth year of analytic treatment, Sarah is doing much better in many ways. She is not as severely depressed or anxious and she has reduced her self-sabotaging patterns. Her difficulty relating to men remains. She has not had a boyfriend or had sex for almost ten years.

There is a theme within the transference that was prominent from the beginning and remains a central thread. Sarah sees me as an intimidating male authority that she wants to receive fatherly guidance from but imagines this will always be given alongside of judgment, sternness, and anger. There is a unique way she relates to me that pulls me into that role. I will make various interpretations that are fairly on the mark, regarding a wide variety of topics. But, soon enough, she will start to say something that either makes her sound naïve, lazy, or forgetful. I will take it up as a matter of common sense and ask her for details. Then, Sarah will offer more details that make her look clueless, stupid, or immature. At that point, I will sometimes end up making some comment about how "it seems obvious that she should have done it this way or that way instead of how she did it."

Sarah will respond by telling me that she didn't think of it or that she forgot. Again, this leads me to feel hopeless about her intelligence and frustrated about her motivations. Indeed, sometimes she tells me she "just didn't feel like it" or "I don't care if it was my fault. I guess I am just lazy". Depending on how she says it, I might feel empathic, want to hear more about it and help her find the solution to whatever the problem was or I might feel like she is being a lazy little brat and want to lecture her on the correct way of proceeding. So, I was caught up in either being an attentive, gentle, guiding father or an irritated, lecturing father. Grinberg (1962) has noted how when put off balance by projective identification, the analyst, can become passively led into acting out various archaic roles within the patient's internal landscape.

By exploring and examining this transference and counter-transference pattern, certain things came to light. It often turns out that Sarah in fact knew exactly what to do in the situation she was describing or indeed had already taken care of whatever it was, but failed to include that detail in her story to me. Exploring this, we have come to see how she successfully provoked me, teased me, or invited me to be like a nice teacher ready to help but easily tipped over into a scolding, impatient teacher. We have explored how this is a repetition of her childhood experience and memory of her father combined with her wish for a different experience or memory. In analyzing this, we have come to realize that it is now her who can be judgmental, impatient, and disappointed with either herself or others and that in the transference she puts me in that role as well. At the same time, she wants to be with a new, more loving man but she feels she must be a helpless, naïve little girl to do so, which then shifts the object back to being a critical and scolding father with her feeling like a disappointing daughter.

More specific to this interpretive enactment pattern with Sarah is the way in which I was duplicating her own defenses and conflicts against seeing herself as competent, independent, and successful without me. The submissive daughter who was linked to me as a faithful father through criticism and expectation was a familiar internal struggle. This was easy to use to defend against and hide from the scarier and unknown relationship of grown woman and man together as equals with her showing her own strengths and opinions.

Over time, by consistently examining and monitoring my counter-transference and my occasional lapses into interpretive acting out, I have been more able to reduce my enactments. And, as we work to learn, understand, and change her father↔child phantasies, there is much less provocative and teasing transference from her to draw me in. In fact, because I have been more aware of the defensive projections that I was interpretively acting out, we both are more open now to her previously warded off feelings of competence and individuality. Sarah now exhibits much more maturity, confidence, and pride. Her stories about her week are much more prone to be about her successes and how she solved various problems. In working through my own counter-transference and projective identification based acting out, I helped Sarah to have less investment in her defensive stance.

Now, Sarah is less conflicted when considering herself as a more independent and vibrant woman linking to me as more of a proud, understanding father who respects his daughter's autonomy and personal choice. Recently, I interpreted that she seems not yet ready to see us an equal adults because she worries she might have to give up all of the nice father/happy daughter gratification she has with me if she becomes a mature, separate woman. Sarah responded by saying, "I am getting there, but even if I can see myself as stronger and more able, the fact is that I still need your help. Sometimes, that feels like a good thing and I like depending on you. Other times, I resent it and feel bad because it reminds me of how much I am still struggling with my life."

In this way, we are having more genuine, important exchanges and less acting out on both sides of the equation.

Case Material

A similar fender bender occurred in my working with Tom. He had been in analytic treatment, on the couch, for several years. He was continuing to explore his pattern of caretaking a woman he had known since high school who was very erratic and was drug addicted. Tom told me he "wanted help in breaking free of this way of being and find a new way of living my life and finding a real girlfriend". This woman was the only girl he had ever had sex with and he felt so poorly about himself that he couldn't picture another woman ever wanting to be with him.

So, I interpreted his sense of power and control over this woman and how he pictured that he alone could rescue her and prevent any harm from coming to her. Genetically, we have linked this to his early experiences with a depressed mother who was institutionalized several times after the death of her second child. Tom recalls how the family reacted with stoic silence and "that everyone said nothing and just pretended everything was ok. We didn't want mom to sink into that dark place again. No one in the family ever talked about their feelings. I thought it was best for mom if I acted nice and made everything smooth". I added, "Or, you might be too much for her, hurt her, and make her depressed". He said yes.

One way this fear and guilt of hurting the object and his need to cater, care, and please the weak, sickly object came into the transference was around the Christmas holiday. A week before the holiday, we were scheduled to meet. He told me he was thinking of going skiing that week and said he assumed I would be taking it off. I told him I would not, that I would be working. When he attended that session, it came out that he didn't really want to be there, but realized I "must be working because I really need the money. You probably need the cash to pay your bills and buy presents for the family". So, out of guilt and obligation, Tom attended the session so he could pay me and prop me up in my desperate financial situation. I interpreted that he saw me as yet another broken down mother who needed protection and care. He told me he was also worried I or the girlfriend would be angry with him and reject him if he "didn't do what he should to meet both of your needs". He added that "she might kill herself if I draw my limits and make my own way".

Over time, I had also been interpreting that he was using her in that he saw her as the one source of sex he could go to and sometimes manipulate into having sex if she felt lonely or was drunk. Here, I was partly exploring his more controlling, sadistic or opportunistic side but also bringing up the level of his desperation and his phantasy of not having access to anyone else due to his conviction of being "too ugly, not masculine, and not a skilled sexual person".

One of the issues that came to light after the first year and after Tom working through a great deal of shame and embarrassment was his chronic masturbation. He tended to masturbate everyday, calling them his trainings. In these "trainings", he tried to escape all the obsessive worries he had about his defectiveness and inferiority. So, by masturbating "properly and successfully", he tried to prove to himself that he was hard enough, could last long enough, had a long enough penis, had properly sized and properly dangling testicles, and that his ejaculations were powerful enough. He had a great deal of worry about all these matters and obsessed about being a failure in every category. This anxiety sometimes grew to near psychotic level in which the anxiety become somatic and somewhat delusional. So, he sometimes ended up going to specialists or even to the emergency room to make sure something wasn't medically wrong when he thought his testicles were not proportional or if there appeared to be a blemish on his penis.

So, recently Tom was telling me about how he was masturbating to a porn site on his computer and how he felt "anxious, pressured, and guilty" about lasting long enough since he was masturbating to a porn star and "she would want it to last a long time". This was an interesting window into the intense phantasy he lived in which sometimes eroded reality to a severe degree, leaving him feeling like he was literally with this porn star and having to literally please her or face the consequences. At first, I was drawn into commenting on his slavish need to please the porn star to avoid her rejection as well as to avoid hurting her feelings and leaving her to become a depressed mother. Again, as with all my previous interpretations that were in line with this theme, I believe I was accurate and helpful. But, I was also missing out on the other side of his conflict, the other aspect of his phantasy. In this way, there was a fender bender. I was pulled into siding with his more masochistic way of relating and his need for me to see him that way. What was being hidden and not noticed or emphasized by either one of us was his sense of power, control, and dominance.

So, I found a way out of the fender bender by interpreting that he was telling me how anxious he was to last long enough to please the porn star but at the same time he was hiding from me the fact that in his mind he was indeed having sex with a famous porn star. In other words, I was now drawing attention to his phantasy of power and sexual success. I interpreted that Tom normally tried to only show me his scared impotent side and now we were discussing his hidden porn star side. Tom replied, "I feel embarrassed, but you are absolutely right. I do have that side but I keep it hidden and secret. But, I have lots of phantasies like that". I asked for details. He told me that a reoccurring image he masturbates to is the picture of a crowd of people around him watching him have sex with a woman and the crowd is amazed at how sexually powerful he is. They are practically cheering him on. And, the woman is begging for more of his incredible sexual prowess.

The next session, Tom reported two dreams. In the first one, he had his cheering crowd and he was the sexual stud. In the second one, he had been rejected by a woman and felt like a "sexual loser". I interpreted that he was very anxious about having exposed this more prideful, masculine side of himself to me and now he was feeling unsure and guilty. In other words, he showed off in front of me in the session and in the dream, but then he had to quickly devalue himself and put himself back down in this inferior place just in case I might be upset with him acting too potent. Tom agreed and talked about feeling "like it was wrong and foolish to think of himself so arrogantly, even though it felt good at the same time". So, now that we were beyond the fender bender, we were able to explore and work on a much fuller, richer portrait of his inner life.

DISCUSSION

Segal (1977) has noted how the patient projects into the analyst's mind, affecting the analyst in certain ways. I would add that the patient attempts to install, infect, control, or reshape the analyst's mind in particular manners that are aggressive, defensive, and reparative. Joseph (1975) has noted how helpful the counter-transference can be in teaching the analyst about how and why the patient is attempting to draw the analyst into various roles and enactments and how and why the patient wants to have a say in the functioning of the analyst's mind. Joseph (1985) has reported on how patients draw us into their defensive systems. This paper has examined this phenomenon as a byproduct of intensive projective identification in which the analyst unwillingly makes interpretations based on this distorted counter-transference experience.

Spillius (1988) and Schafer (1994) have pointed out how various Kleinian thinkers including Rosenfeld (1987) have clinically found how patients hope for the analyst to be able to have the capacity to remain stable and dependable when confronted with projections. However, these same patients usually are very anxious about the analyst's ability to remain stable, neutral, and integrated so the patient may retreat, repair, or altogether avoid putting the analyst in the dangerous position of having to contain their projections in the first place. One way this occurs is that the patient projects their defensive system into the analyst as a way to help the analyst avoid being toppled or injured or overwhelmed when encountering the true self of the patient. This also protects the patient from feeling potential persecution or guilt from inserting their various conflicts and phantasies into the analyst. The case material has illustrated how some patients project various levels of defense and denial into the analyst to protect both self and object from more individual, independent, and successful aspects of the self as well as difference, disagreement, or separation and growth. At times, the analyst can be drawn into acting out these defenses systems by interpreting only one aspect of the patient's dynamics rather than other aspects. The inferior or immature aspects of the patient can become over emphasized rather than the growing, challenging, or superior feelings and phantasies. In this way, both analyst and patient collude in a defensive role relationship designed to focus on old, pathological ways of being rather than new, transformative ways of relating. By monitoring the counter-transference and the interpretive acting out that occurs in these situations, the analyst can begin to regain analytic balance, disengage from therapeutic fender benders, and come back from these projective identification based counter-transference detours onto the road to change and emotional clarity.

Summary

The day to day work that the psychoanalytic endeavor demands on both patient and analyst typically involves an ongoing series of successes and failures with various ups and downs. There is clarity and mystery within each session as well as over the course of an entire treatment. Hopefully, these breakdowns and breakthroughs are mixed together and balanced more toward the gradual working through and transformation of unconscious conflict and psychological suffering. Often, there is more of a murky series of confusing detours that often bring us to something helpful and important, but with a great deal of entanglements along the way.

Most of our patients in private practice or clinic settings are fairly disturbed and coping in a fairly raw, slippery, or confusing manner. It is common to become involved in counter-transference acting out and temporarily lost in intense projective identification cycles in which the patient subtly or dramatically pulls the analyst into a variety of roles.

Sandler (1976) has noted that the concept of transference should be broadened to include not just the projections of archaic figures from the past, but all the patient's attempts to manipulate or provoke certain role relationships with the analyst. Sandler goes on to say that the patient unconsciously scans the analyst's reactions to their projections to assess if the analyst can handle it or not and to see if the analyst is choosing to take up a certain side of things over another. The patient's ability to accurately perceive this is of course distorted by the hopes and dread of their unconscious phantasy. The patients examined in this paper are scanning the analyst to see if the object is capable and willing to accept and tolerate the more independent and assertive side of their phantasies. But, because of intense internal convictions regarding the frail, rejecting, angry, or disapproving aspects of the object, the patient is quick to assume rejection or collapse. So, they are quick to project certain defenses against the side of themselves and emphasize or promote the view of themselves as quite opposite. These are what Sandler calls the defensive role relationships that are constructed to manipulate the analyst away from these areas perceived as dangerous to either self or object. Once the analyst takes on a part of this defensive construction, the counter-transference, the counter-transference reactions are played out in the manner in which interpretations are given. Even thought the bulk of the interpretive process may still seem on target and helpful in assisting the patient to work through many different conflicts, it is also a one-sided approach and is a blind spot of sorts in which the analyst is now avoiding the same feelings or transference anxiety that the patient is avoiding.

Now, one could say the interpretive acting out is a sign of therapeutic failure. On the other hand, Money-Kryle (1956) has noted that it is common for the analyst to fail in their function as a container. But, the specifics of how he fails can be very informative. Thus, the ongoing monitoring of how counter-transference and projective identification is contaminating the interpretive process should be a regular part of the analyst's evaluation of self and object. The manner in which the interpretive process has gone astray or askew points to the area of the patient's mind that is manipulating, hiding, rebelling, or retreating.

Another way the patient may draw the analyst into a defensive structure that only illuminates certain aspects of their personality while cloaking others is to carefully strip away the knowledge and insight from the analyst's interpretations. Joseph (1989) has noted how this can stimulate more of a sadomasochistic transference and counter-transference situation in which the patient denies more and more of himself which provokes interpretive attacks or devaluations from the analyst. Therefore, neither party has to acknowledge the more positive, growth orientated, or differentiated aspects of the patient. The motive for this projective identification driven defensive stance can be to prevent or escape either paranoid (Klein 1946) or depressive (Klein 1935; 1940) fears.

Grinberg (1979) notes that when under the passive sway of intense projective identification forces, the analyst can become drawn into various roles affects and phantasies which he may play out with the patient in different ways. Grinberg goes on to describe a classification of projective identification states that include specific aims, contents, and effects on others. Central to the patient's I am examining in this paper, Grinberg notes the controlling and evacuative and defensive aims combined with the superego functions that have confusioning and defensive effects on the analyst.

The patients presented in this paper are representative of those individuals who are haunted by paranoid (Klein 1946), pre-depressive (Bicudo 1964; Grinberg 1964), and depressive (Klein 1935; 1940) anxieties regarding separation, differentiation, growth, and change. For these individuals, change equals danger (Waska 2006). Torras De Bea (1989) has noted how differentiation is from birth the essential element in projective identification that is based around unconscious self to object communication. However, when this natural and pervasive communication is distorted or perverted by anxieties regarding unacceptable, to self and/or object, acts of differentiation, massive defenses are brought up and become the core of projective identification. The elements of projection shift from more of a communication process to a rigid defensive maneuver designed to hide or destroy any evidence of change, challenge, separation or growth. Of course, this enters the realm of masochistic camouflage, the death instinct, and various forms of negative therapeutic reaction.

The analyst's interpretive function must be restored in order to begin re-establishing analytic contact (Waska 2007) and to begin helping the patient deal with the anxiety they are defending against. Once the counter-transference reaction becomes less of an acting out via interpretation and more of an informative toll, then the analyst can start to investigate the unconscious elements of the patient's projective identification efforts. Heimann (1950) has noted that the analyst needs to always be curious about why the patient is currently, in the moment, doing what to whom in phantasy, to either self or other. All transference interpretations come forth from this equation. This paper has outlined the ways the analyst can be caught up in the projective identification cycle of defensive maneuvers that create counter-transference induced interpretive blind spots.

Riesenberg-Malcolm (1995) has discussed the core importance of the transference relationship as the what, the paranoid or depressive level of conflict as the where, and the when being the verbal integration of interpretive elements at a particular moment when things gel in the mind of the analyst. These critical interpretive ingredients are all susceptible to this projective identification and counter-transference blind spot. In particular, the analyst may be drawn into one aspect of the patient's internal conflict while avoiding another, therefore only aware of a lopsided picture of the transference relationship. As a result, it might appear to be a paranoid or depressive problem when it is not necessarily so. Finally, these fake or only partly true clinical facts will prevent, distort, or rush the moment when pre-interpretive elements gel in the analyst's mind.

Joseph (1988; 1989) has shown in her extensive clinical focus the way the analyst is almost always drawn into playing out a role in the patient's phantasies. If the analyst can maintain an observing stance and not be pulled too deeply into these interpretive enactments (Steiner 2006), the analyst can be better informed as to the patient's defensive structure and the conflicts he has regarding his object relational world. Our job involves being the willing recipient of the patient's ongoing projections which by definition clouds our ability to reason and think. However, it is imperative to our ability to contain and translate to be able to think on our feet. So, there is always a difficult and confusing place we must reside, trying to understand rather than act, yet the patient's projections constantly pull us toward action.

Joseph (1989) has discussed the concept of psychic equilibrium and how the patient strives to maintain what may appear to be a malfunction and pathological system of coping to avoid a lack of psychic balance with their internal objects and a shift into an internal state of unknown difference and change. Projective identification can be utilized to maintain this rigid equilibrium and to keep those objects, including the transference object of the analyst, from seeing any evidence of ambition, differentiation, or psychological growth.

Joseph (2003) and Steiner (2006) have both written about the enactment process as it takes place within the interpretive field. Steiner (2006) points out the limiting or even destructive effects interpretive acting out can have on the patient's ability to develop their own thinking and judgment. He goes on to point out how the analyst has to keep his feelings under control, remaining both involved and separate, in order to be engaged, but also able to observe and assess. This paper has illustrated both the limiting effects of interpretive acting out as well as the informative and therapeutic aspects of examining, exploring, and utilizing the unconscious foundation of these often unavoidable dynamics.

REFERENCES

Bicudo, V. (1964). Persecutory Guilt and Ego Restrictions—Characterization of a Pre-Depressive Position. *International Journal of Psycho-Analysis, 45,* 358-363.

Brenman, P. (1985). Working Through the Counter-Transference, *International Journal of Psychoanalysis*, *66*, 157-166.

De Bea, T. (1989). Projective Identification and Differentiation. *International Journal of Psycho-Analysis*, *70*, 265-274.

Grinberg, L. (1962). On a Specific Aspect of Countertransference Due to the Patient's Projective Identification. *International Journal of Psycho-Analysis* *43*, 436-440.

Grinberg, L. (1964). Two Kinds of Guilt—their Relations with Normal and Pathological Aspects of Mourning. *International Journal of Psycho-Analysis* *45*, 366-371.

Grinberg, L. (1979). Counter-transference and Projective Counter-Identification, *Contemporary Psychoanalysis*, *15*, 226-247.

Heimann, P. (1950). On Counter-Transference. *International Journal of Psycho-Analysis*, *31*, 81-84.

Hinshelwood, R. (1989). A Dictionary of Kleinian Thought, Jason Aronson, New York.

Joseph, B. (1975). The Patient Who is Difficult to Reach, In *Tactics and Techniques in Psychoanalytic Therapy*, *Volume 2*: Countertransference (Eds.) P. L. Giovacchini. New York: Jason Aronson Inc., 205-216.

Joseph, B. (1985). Transference: The Total Situation. *International Journal of Psycho-Analysis*, *66*, 447-454.

Joseph, B. (1988). Object Relations in Clinical Practice, *Psychoanalytic Quarterly*, *57*, 626-640.

Joseph, B. (1989). Psychic Equilibrium and Psychic Change, London, Routledge

Joseph, B. (2003). *Ethics and Enactment, Psychoanalysis Eur*, *57*, 147-153.

Money-Kyrle, R. (1956). Normal Counter-Transference and Some of its Deviations. *International Journal of Psycho-Analysis*, *37*, 360-366.

Klein, M. (1935). A Contribution to the Psychogenesis of Manic-Depressive States. *International Journal of Psycho-Analysis*, *16*, 145-174.

Klein, M. (1940). Mourning and its Relation to Manic-Depressive States. *International Journal of Psycho-Analysis*, *21*, 125-153.

Klein, M. (1946). Notes on Some Schizoid Mechanisms. *International Journal of Psycho-Analysis*, *27*, 99-110.

Riesenberg-Malcolm, R. (1995). The Three "W's": What, Where, and When: The Rational of Interpretation, *International Journal of Psychoanalysis*, *76*, 447.

Rosenfeld, H. (1971). A Clinical Approach to the Psychoanalytic Theory of the Life and Death Instincts: An Investigation Into the Aggressive Aspects of Narcissism. *International Journal of Psycho-Analysis*, *52*, 169-178.

Rosenfeld, H. (1987). *Impasse and Interpretations*, Tavistock, London.

Sandler, J. (1976). Counter-Transference and Role Responsiveness, *International Journal of Psychoanalysis, 3*,43.

Segal, H. (1977). Counter-transference, *International Journal of Psychoanalysis, 6*, 31-37.

Schafer, R. (1994). The Contemporary Kleinians of London. *Psychoanalytic Quarterly, 63*, 409-432.

Spillius, E. (1988). Melanie Klein Today: *Developments in Theory and Practice. Volume I*: Mainly Theory, London and New York: Routledge.

Steiner, J. (1987). Interplay between Pathological Organizations and the Paranoid-Schizoid and Depressive Positions, *International Journal of Psychoanalysis, 68*, 69-80.

Steiner, J. (1993). Psychic Retreats: Pathological Organizations in Psychotic, *Neurotic and Borderline Patients*, Routledge.

Steiner, J. (2006). Interpretive Enactments and the Analytic Setting, *International Journal of Psychoanalysis, 87*, 2, 315-320.

Waska, R. (2006). *The Danger of Change: The Kleinian Approach with Patients who Experience Progress as Trauma*, Brunner/Rutledge, London.

Waska, R. (2006). The Analyst as Translator, *Psychoanalytic Social Work, 13*,43-65.

Waska, R. (2007). *The Concept of Analytic Contact: A Kleinian Approach to Reaching the Hard to Reach Patient*, Brunner/Rutledge, London.

In: Psychology of Hate
Editors: Carol T. Lockhardt, pp.103-119

Chapter 5

DO YOU HATE ME? HAVE I HURT YOU?: DEFENSES AGAINST GROWTH, SEPARATION, AND INDIVIDUATION THAT CREATE INTERPRETIVE ENACTMENTS PART TWO: PIT STOPS AND THE SHARED DEFENSIVE SYSTEMS OF MORE DIFFICULT PATIENTS

Robert Waska[*]

Institute for Psychoanalytic Studies,
Private Psychoanalytic Practice in San Francisco
and Marin County, CA, USA

ABSTRACT

Some more disturbed patients in psychoanalytic treatment are struggling with primitive depressive anxieties and conflicts regarding separation and individuation. They feel obligated to follow what they believe their object needs, wants, or demands while at the same time feeling restricted and wanting to oppose or reject those needs for their own ambitions and choices.

[*] Corresponding author: E-mail: drwaska@aol.com, Telephone: 415-883-4235, P.O. Box 2769 San Anselmo, CA 94979 USA

However, the phantasy of rejection and punishment as well as lasting harm to their object results in great conflict and a sense of entrapment. So, the patient is left with feeling they will create hate and harm if they admit their own needs, differences, accomplishments. Thus, these differentiation and individuation states are cloaked and camouflaged. While working with such patients, the analyst frequently is subject to projective identification attacks in which the patient's defenses against change, growth, separation, and individual choice become acted out in the interpretive field. Two cases are used for illustration and the need for careful counter-transference monitoring is discussed.

INTRODUCTION

Some more disturbed patients in psychoanalytic treatment are struggling with primitive depressive anxieties and conflicts regarding separation and individuation. They feel obligated to follow what they believe their object needs, wants, or demands while at the same time feeling restricted and wanting to oppose or reject those needs for their own ambitions and choices. However, the phantasy of rejection and punishment as well as lasting harm to their object results in great conflict and a sense of entrapment. So, the patient is left with feeling they will create hate and harm if they admit their own needs, differences, accomplishments. Thus, these differentiation and individuation states are cloaked and camouflaged. While working with such patients, the analyst frequently is subject to projective identification attacks in which the patient's defenses against change, growth, separation, and individual choice become acted out in the interpretive field. Two cases are used for illustration and the need for careful counter-transference monitoring is discussed.

Heimann (1950) was among the first in the Kleinian school who emphasized the utility of counter-transference as opposed to viewing it as a personal liability. She explained that one of the benefits of our own analysis is being able to sustain our feelings as opposed to discharging them like the patient does. In sustaining our feelings, we can examine them in relation to what the patient is saying, feeling, or doing and begin to expand our understanding of the internal conflicts our patient is working with.

Money-Kyrle (1956) and Bion (1959) discussed the importance of acting as a container for the patient's projections by tolerating them and by putting those projections into words. I see this process as becoming a psychic translator and psychological filter for the patient's unknown, unwanted, and unthinkable thoughts, feelings, and phantasies. Through this way of working and Klein's

(1946) concept of projective identification, the analyst was now able to make intra-psychic interpretations of the interpersonal interactions in the clinical moment, bringing insight into the total transference (Joseph 1985).

Due to these Kleinian discoveries and advances in clinical technique, the analyst is now able to better assist the patient with his anxiety and psychological confusion. The analyst takes in the intra-psychic meaning of interpersonal interactions, using the counter-transference as an organizing tool to decode the interactive projection, and then eventually interprets the core conflicts that make that interaction up, offering the patient a potentially mutative experience. Of course, in using counter-transference to better understand the patient, the analyst has to become acutely aware of how he reacts to the patient's projections. A common reaction to various forms of aggression, envy, demand, separation, individuation, loss, or seduction is to move away defensively. The standing task in examining counter-transference is to determine if that defensive reaction is the analyst's own personal retaliation or the patient's unique personal defensive structure that is being pushed into the analyst.

The patient may be quite anxious about the analyst's view of usually hidden parts of the self, convinced the analyst could feel the same judgment that the patient harbors about certain aspects of his own personality which are normally kept hidden, repressed, or split off. So, the patient can become very anxious, either in a paranoid-schizoid (Klein 1946) or depressive (Klein 1935, 1940) manner, about what will happen when the object realizes the patient's true identity, mindset, or affect state.

Therefore, it is very common for the patient to use projective identification to push various forms of defense into the analyst which becomes embedded within how the analyst acts or interprets. Then, the analyst can end up colluding with the patient to deny, avoid, or minimize what the patient imagines to be offensive, toxic, taboo, or unwanted. The two cases in this paper will illustrate how the analyst can become over focused on one aspect of the patient's transference or phantasy state as part of a defensive acting out of this type of projective identification dynamic. The analyst's interpretations are only helpful or mutative when the analyst works to contain himself and translates his counter-transference feelings in a way that makes himself separate and different than the patient's archaic internal objects (Elmhirst 1978).

Projective identification influenced counter-transference acting out commonly occurs in the interpretive process when the analyst holds on possessively to the projections or tries to discharge them prematurely. When acting out the patient's defensive dynamics against certain transference anxieties, the analyst is frequently over emphasizing or prematurely interpreting one side of the patient's transference, phantasy state, or internal conflict, while withholding and underemphasizing other aspects.

PIT STOPS: A MOMENTARY BREAK BEFORE DIVING BACK INTO THE FRAY

Pit stops are those clinical situations in which patients come to see us for a brief period, usually in a state of external crisis which is a reflection of intense internal crisis. They desperately want help, hope for immediate change, and seek fast relief. But, they are captured within intense inner conflicts and rigid projective identification systems in which they cry out for the object, flee from the object, grieve for the object, and move to attack and fight the object. The anger, guilt, loss, and fear towards themselves and others seem at unbearable levels and rapidly vacillating cycles. These shifting phantasies regarding love, hate, and knowledge make for chaotic, short, and taxing treatments. Like fender benders, the analyst may play some counter-transference role in enacting various pathological phantasies with the patient. However, even when the analyst maintains or regains a balanced and measured analytic stance, this group of patients are very difficult, hard to reach, and prone to fragmentation and flight.

If we realize that these momentary brushes with the analytic process is all that the patient can handle or will allow at that given period in their life, we may be able to help them to some modest degree. This may be to bring them back to a pathological state they are used to before they entered the current crisis or it may be the chance to establish analytic contact long enough to given them a taste of internal choice, peace, or freedom which they have never before experienced. Even if this is only fleeting, it still may act as a seed for some point later in time where they might make another pit stop or fender bender in which they might find some degree of healing and growth.

Case Material

Liz came to see me after "feeling on the verge of a breakdown" at her new job of six months. She was the youngest of several children raised by "loving parents who have always been there for us". Liz described an upper-middle class lifestyle of boarding schools where she excelled in her studies and as a member of the track team where she trained everyday for several hours and helped the school win various awards.

She said her parents were loving and attentive but that when her father had taken to drinking he was "angry and impossible to talk with for much of my early teen years". Liz is now twenty-six years old and still very close to her family. She relies on them for guidance and help in most matters. Her father gave up drinking years ago so they "have a very good relationship now" but Liz still "gets fed up with him sometimes".

In college, Liz excelled at her classes and was on several sports teams. She told me she could see looking back how "she worked very hard and was extremely focused but that it was all for something she believed in and enjoyed so it didn't seem like a burden."

After graduating with high marks in her business degree, Liz was offered several prestigious jobs. One was locally, near her family, working with local charity organizations to help develop new approaches to serving the poor. Liz wanted to take the job and said it "felt right and was very exciting. I would be really hands on taking my business skills to the streets and actually making a difference." The other offer was from a major corporate law firm across the country. She was also excited about this opportunity but was unsure what to do. Liz's father and several other family members told her to "Go for the big bucks. It is a perfect career with enormous earning potential". She felt they "were probably right " and they said they would help me out in whatever way I needed so to just try it out and know the family is backing you".

So, six months ago Liz moved out to the West Coast to begin her new corporate job. She had no friends or relatives in the area and had only met a few executives at the company during the interview process. She began working in a highly demanding, high stress environment in which a typical day was 12-15 hours with no real lunch break. Very soon, she was taking home at night and coming into work on Sundays. When I asked about this, in response to her telling me things were "pretty stressful", she immediately told me that "type of schedule is pretty standard in the industry, everyone does it".

Liz told me about being tired all the time and never having any time to herself. She was looking more exhausted and depressed. Thus, pulled by my counter-transference of not feeling like I would ever put up with this situation and therefore neither should she, I asked her about what was so difficult about setting limits. Here, my question was important and relevant but it would have been better if I had interpreted how she was presenting all the tired stories but never adding anything about wanting limits and therefore she seemed to want to have me step in and set them for her. Instead, I was playing out a projective identification based transference phantasy. Another way of viewing this dynamic is that I was quickly part of an Oedipal triangle in which there was the job, Liz, and I. She would show allegiance to one and then the other. I found myself fighting against one for the benefit of the other.

I felt pulled to be a good father stepping in to set limits on her behalf, teach her how to say no, and encourage her to take care of herself instead of be a slave to her job. But, when I acted this out in a modest degree, I noticed that Liz now turned away from her despair and exhaustion to a multitude of concrete reasons why she had to work under those conditions, how it was normal, and how everyone did it. So, one interpretation was to point out how she wanted me to be the good, soothing father who would set limits for her. Now, I also interpreted that she was reacting to that wish and turning into a stern, matter of fact father who was explaining to me how there is work to be done and that is just the way it is. At one point, she turned to talking about trying to "do her best" and "not let anyone down". This last statement was a masochistic rise to excellence that had to occur regardless of how tired or unhappy she was. I interpreted her want to please me, her boss, and her father no matter what and she was going to show us all what a hard working good little girl she was even if that meant sacrificing her own needs.

So, very quickly in Liz's analytic treatment, she illustrated her need to use work and performance in general as a retreat from her worries of judgment and her never ending struggle to win over her objects. Up to the point of this new job, it appeared that Liz had successfully used excelling and "doing her best" as a defense against various depressive anxieties and some more primitive paranoid fears. In her mind, over achieving had always left her feeling accepted, loved, and victorious. But, the demands of this new career and her lack of interest in the work itself created a fragile psychic retreat that was springing multiple leaks. She tried to shore these up by working harder and increasing her level of denial about her true feelings and instead justifying her focused dedication with logic about industry standards.

Liz's object relational conflicts were intense. On one hand, there was her desire to please her father and not fail what she saw as her obligation to follow his guidance. So, when I tried to be compassionate and helpful, Liz heard that as me encouraging her to disappoint her father/boss. When I made this interpretation, she felt able to speak about the other side of her conflict. She told me how she was "angry with her father for always telling her what to do and then expecting her to like it and excel at it". After she discussed this for awhile, I interpreted that while this may be true, it also looked like she was now being her demanding father all by herself, exacting long hours and no time for personal enjoyment. For a moment she reflected and took this in and told me she thought "it was accurate and useful". But then she said, "But I want to know what exactly to do to begin working on this problem". I pointed out that she in a bossy, demanding way was now making me into her boss/father and wanting my instructions on her next assignment. This sort of interaction led me to think she was very unsure of what would happen if she gave up this fixed, strict approach to life. I interpreted that she did not want to give up the chance to be the best but hated that she had no choice in the matter when under her own strict fatherly demands for excellence. To give herself a chance and see what she might want instead felt like a frightening disappointment to her objects and a turning toward an unknown new way of being where she felt no control and no one to turn herself over to. Liz said she thought she wanted to try this out but wasn't sure what the "right decision was yet".

The stress of trying to please this projection of a highly demanding and never satiated father object left Liz collapsed and depressed. She lost weight, looked haggard, and developed stomach problems. Now, she spend what little free time she had either going to gastro specialists for tests or trying to rest. This was difficult as she was working fifteen hour days now. Finally, the physical manifestations of her cruel and constant demand on herself took its toll. She was so exhausted and sick that she had to take two weeks off and stayed in bed most of the time except to see me or her other medical specialists. Again, she separated this problem out in a concrete fashion and saw it as a stomach problem not related to either her job, her father, or her emotional conflicts.

Over the next month, the stress of her psychological issues created even greater problems. Liz became increasingly depressed and anxious under the burden of tolling away at something she felt she had to excel at even though she "didn't really see the point of most of the work, it is boring and repetitive". At one point, Liz said she hated it was close to quitting. But, at the same time, showing the degree of internal conflict she struggle with, Liz told me she didn't want to disappoint her boss. She continued reacting to her desire to quit by saying, "maybe I just need to get into the swing of things, put my head down, and stop complaining. I should realize life is not supposed to be a bowl of cherries". The bit about not wanting to disappoint her boss rang a bell for me as Liz had mentioned several times how she felt obligated to go with whatever her father recommended and not let him down. She said he is "always very supportive and freely gives me advise". Liz said she is often unsure about how to proceed in life so she will ask him what to do and always takes his suggestions. I interpreted that she wants his love and approval and has decided she should do what he says and not disappoint him or she will loose this precious commodity. But, that puts her in a spot of having no choice of her own without feeling very guilty. So, she has to become an angry victim to what she now sees as either his unreasonable demands or her own pathetic incompetence. I interpreted that she has a mind of her own and some ideas of what she wants to do, but is anxious that if I find out I will be disappointed or disapprove. She would be turning away from me and father, leaving her feeling guilty, lonely, and scared of reprisal. So, she doubles her efforts to "be the best" and please me, her boss, her father, and her own internal slave driver rather than to be herself and cause trouble and face the consequences. Here, I was interpreting the core anxiety behind the projective identification defenses she was utilizing.

Liz responded, "I am very angry with my father. He always tells me to go for it, do whatever it is, like moving out here and taking this job. He says he will always be there for me and support me. But, I feel totally left alone. I did it for him in a way and now I regret it sometimes. But, I don't want to be a quitter. What do I do?!" Here, Liz was able to access and share a formally split off conflict around her relationship with father. She wants to please him and wants to feel his supportive love in exchange. But, she feels he has betrayed her and she in turn is sick of doing what he wants instead of what she wants. As soon as she expresses this warded off feeling, she becomes conflicted and guilty. She sees herself as a "quitter" if she stops catering to father. But, she wants to feel more independent as well. Then, she jettisons the conflict into me and demands, "what do I do?" Here, she wants me to become her father and tell her what to do.

I made that interpretation and Liz said, "I see what you mean, but I don't want to have to make the decision myself". I interpreted that she uses me as a father to avoid and the guilt and anxiety of being her own boss but then would feel trapped by my fatherly advice. I said, "from everything you tell me and how you describe your work, it seems clear you want to quit and find something you will enjoy instead of trying to appease your father, your boss, and myself. But, you are such a taskmaster that you feel guilty and like a quitter so you don't want to admit wanting more freedom and independence. You would rather have me tell you to quit your job than face your own desires about it." Here, I was interpreting the projective identification process that shaped her transference. Instead of acting out her projected defenses in the form of interpretive enactment, I was able to clearly spell out her unconscious struggles and fears around love, hate, and growth. Liz responded by telling me she should "just find a way to be more efficient and work smarter. Everyone else in the office doesn't seem to have a problem. I should stop whining." I said, "You are suddenly reacting to my idea that you have your own feelings and wishes. You are saying you are simply lazy and need to work harder. Now, you are acting like how you see your father and you want me to fight him and disagree with him". So, I was now interpreting her rapid cycling between being the demanding father, the desperate child, and the stubborn child who will prove she can do it. At the same time, Liz was shifting her phantasy view of me in accordance to each self/object perspective.

Unfortunately, Liz's health continued to deteriorate and she became more depressed. Her coworkers noticed and her boss suggested she go on a medical leave. I think she took this as her father giving her permission to stop working at a job she hated. So, she informed me by phone that she was leaving the next week to be with her family for several months and thanked me for my services.

While her treatment was short and rocky, I believe we did accomplish something positive given the circumstances. While I initially was pulled into an interpretive acting out of some of Liz's defenses against differentiation and growth, I was able to find my therapeutic footing and help her address some of her core conflicts and internal anxieties.

Many patients show up to our offices in similar states of crisis, anxiety, and urgency. They leave fairly soon afterwards for various reasons. But, if we strive to make and maintain analytic contact with them, there can be a degree of help, integration, or change. Perhaps we can only offer a mild support and balance for them but this may be all they can take in at that time. We can still help them learn about themselves and create a sense of hope or curiosity. Some of these short term cases take a quick pit stop on our couches before resuming the precarious race they are in. For others, this pit stop is the first step in realizing they have a choice to step out of that race and into something new and nourishing, something they can author instead of feeling passive and victimized. We strive to illuminate the patient's unconscious object relational world, gradually providing the patient a way to understand, express, translate, and master their previously unbearable thoughts and feelings. We make contact it their deepest experiences so they can make contact with their fullest potential.

Case Material

Edward was told by his company to seek therapy and find out why he always stayed at work past the time when everyone went home, why he kept garbage and old food containers around his desk even though his manager asked him to not do that, and why he insisted on doing certain projects for the company which no one ever asked for. This last point was also part of a conflict in which Edward insisted he knew what was best for the company's "wellbeing" and felt compelled to take action on these projects even when no one asked or even if someone said not to.

He was caught sleeping at his desk several times because of how late he stayed there everyday. From what I could gather, he had been with the company for so long that they tolerated his odd behavior for many years but a new manager would not tolerate it. In fact, it sounded like the company was trying to fire him and actually they did tell him if he continued with his current behavior they would.

Edward appeared disorganized and low functioning, but intellectually sharp. He was obese and disheveled, with his underwear hanging out the back, his shirt untucked, and three pairs of glasses hanging off his neck. Over the next few weeks, I noticed he wore the same clothes every time I saw him. Every pants pocket, shirt pocket, and jacket pocket was crammed full of envelopes and pieces of paper. I asked him about that and he told me it "was his filing system and that he kept his mail, mostly unopened, in this filing system.

Edward was extremely anxious and scattered as he talked and was prone to rambling and unlinked topics. He told me how stupid his manager was and "how the manager doesn't realize by making me waste time coming here I am not at work making sure everything runs smoothly".

While Edward was definitely functioning at a psychotic level, he was also extremely smart and knew how to figure out certain systems and projects at work that made him a valuable worker for many years. He company had tolerated his odd ways for many years but now a new manager and tough economic times meant Edward was seen as a liability to be gotten rid of.

Over a period of several months, I listened to a pattern of feelings and thoughts that I attempted to interpret. The main theme I interpreted was that Edward tried to keep his company going on, functioning properly, no matter what. He stayed there till midnight many nights and came back at 6am. As a result, his apartment was so unkempt and full of debris that his landlord was ready to evict him. In fact, that is what happened to his last apartment. I felt, in the counter-transference, that he was desperately trying to keep the company alive, with a sense of single handed power and control and desperation, as if he was the sole lifeguard on a treacherous beach which he had to guard 24/7. I made this interpretation and he responded very concretely, agreeing that yes, this was the case.

When I began hearing about Edward's upbringing, this pattern made some sense. He told me, "Your type, the psycho doctors, like to hear about the mother and the father. Well, I am not sure I want to trust you. It has never been helpful to trust anyone as far as I can tell. History is a showcase for reality. I would rather seek out the outer world and the edge of the grid as it is called by the survivalists. They seem to have some genuine ideas of how to live and avoid the traps. But, right now I have to work and save money so I could do that one day. If I get fired,

I may do that. But, for now, I must make sure the company stays intact, for their own good. They don't know they need me but if I was gone they would quickly see what a mess things become. No one seems to ever care until it is too late. Where was I? Oh. You may want to know about my family but will you only stare at me like all the rest?"

I said, "You are sure I will judge you. Maybe the things you want to share make you anxious and guilty?" Edward said, "If you judge me, it will be a secret you put in your little book. People seem to either keep their thoughts hidden or they come right out and feel they can call themselves superior. I was surprised when they spit on me in high school but no one else seemed surprised. I don't have a good feeling about this". I said, "You are starting to share something very difficult, painful. Let's take it slow and talk about what you are feeling".

Slowly over time, Edward told me about being one of two children raised by an alcoholic and psychotic mother. He said, "Sometimes, she would go crazy and beat us. Other times, she was super depressed and suicidal. I came home from school one day and found her in a puddle of blood after she tried to kill herself. Later, my father yelled at me for not keeping a good watch on her. He wanted me to always keep an eye on her and make sure nothing bad ever happened. He told me I had failed and it was my fault." I asked where his father was when all this was happening. Edward replied, "He was always at work and never home so we had to take care of everything".

Here, I listened closely and interpreted, "that was so painful and scary. You did your best to care for her but it was never enough. You were a kid, she had severe problems, and you ended up feeling responsible for her health. Maybe that is what you are feeling at work, trying to keep the company alive too". Edward responded, "Yes. I am, they need me and no one else knows all the ends and outs". So, he replied to my interpretation of his emotional repetition of caretaking his suicidal and out of control mother with a very concrete view.

Edward seemed to fluctuate between trusting me and then seeing me "as a part of the system, pieces of a puzzle destined for collapse because of manipulation and blind ambition". When he relaxed a bit and saw me as on his side, he shared "his real knowledge of the true layers of life". He told me he was "in touch with many hidden messages and signs that appear in life if you know how to notice them". He told me he had been sent certain messages, "probably from certain Gods, maybe a Goddess". These messages came before the 9/11 terrorist attacks and he didn't recognized them completely or their significance. Therefore, I said, "So, you must feel terrible that you could have maybe stopped the attacks but you didn't realize the essence of the messages". He agreed and said now, looking back, he can see that he was being used as a "conduit" for certain "celestial bodies, perhaps the Greek goddess I mentioned, who provides a window into time and space for reasons that are important to the individual and humanity as well". I interpreted "you must feel a great burden to have to hold all that important information" and thought to myself that this was similar to him having to take care of the company and similar to his phantasy of wanting to predict, prevent, avoid, and heal his mother's suicidal and aggressive behaviors, but ending up feeling to blame somehow.

After a few sessions, I asked Edward if he was dating anyone. He laughed and said, "After that bitch, how could I ever get near anyone. I just want to get away from people, that is my mission in life". He told me, "I know you are just waiting for this, it is what they train you to do. How will you react? I don't know if I can trust you but you probably won't stop asking. I said, "This is very difficult. Tell me what you can and also tell me why it is so hard to trust me".

Edward then proceeded to explain how from ages 10-18 years old his mother preyed on him sexually. She would come into his room at night to fondle him, masturbated him in the car, and kissed him inappropriately before he went off school in the morning. He was clearly anxious telling me this and said, "She was like a mechanical vulture, flexing her metal claws and biting into me with a sharp seriated beak." The way he said this gave me a sudden scare as if he was changing into something dangerous. This was a difficult moment in which I believe projective identification threw me off balance, giving me a taste of mother becoming psychotic and aggressive. He was in a momentary psychotic fusion state with mother and I was pulled along for the ride.

The sexual trauma left Edward with very distorted and contorted images that provided a primitive method of understanding the frightening objects that he was populated by. An example was when he told me about the Greek myth of a "sexy woman who was found out to be a murderess. She seduces you and then turns on you, ripping you apart and leaving your entrails for the wolves". I interpreted, "feeling your mother turned from someone you wanted to look up to and love into a monster is very disturbing". Edward replied, "I have spent my life trying to escape people and only want to be left alone in peace." I said, "It is hard to trust me. You want to but you think I might judge you". He said, "I don't want to just quit my job and let everyone down. I would be lying to them just like people lied to me when they said to just ignore them spitting on you, picking on you, and calling you names".

Edward's idea of a special woman, who was a goddess and might be either good or bad, but held great power, was part of his thinking in many ways. He told me he thought there were "important clues that are left throughout time for those who can recognize and believe". He told me he "has noticed in certain news stories over the years and in certain novels he has read of a pattern or theme regarding a certain type of woman who is special and may be linked to important world situations".

Besides work, Edward did almost nothing. He did not socialize or go out. But, he had a few specific interests. He told me he liked to read comic books and was currently very interested in following a series of stories "about a seemingly ordinary girl who seems very regular and peaceful. But, we are starting to find out, only slowly and somewhat ominously, that she has a certain shadow life. It is turning out that she may actually be the mysterious anti-hero who slays dragons at night. There is no concrete evidence that she has killed a dragon yet, but it is starting to point in that direction". Here, I thought he was telling me about his internal confusion about his objects. Were they normal and peaceful, were they suddenly turning into something else, and was that something else wonderful and protective or sinister and deadly. Also, I thought he wanted to grow out of his ordinary self into a stronger person who could stand up against the dragon but he felt anxious. He might be a hero or he might be a villain killing off an innocent dragon. Here, I thought he might feel this was the dangerous urge he had to be independent and separate, to differentiate, or to express his angry feelings instead of always being the helper.

In general, Edward felt he had always been taken advantage of by all the authorities he had ever looked up to. I interpreted, "I wonder if it is just a matter of time before you see me that way. Or, is there a way for us to build some trust?" He replied, "I am still assessing that". I interpreted that he was trying to make sense out of his mother's crazy behavior, trying to repair her in his mind, and control things at the company that seemed out of control. He felt he had to stand watch over mother and work. He said, "That is an interesting way of thinking. I like that. I will consider it." During one session, he told me, "I feel good about sharing with you; it is a new experience even though I don't really think much of the process". Later in the same session, he said, "I don't know how this could ever help. It is useless". I interpreted his fear of exploring these painful and frightening feelings and memories and trying to trust me". He agreed to "keep trying it for awhile".

Unfortunately, Edward was fired from his company and then told me, "I am not coming back. I don't want to spend my money on this. I may look for another job or I may just see about moving away, somewhere far away like the survivalists who live off the land, maybe to Montana or somewhere else where there is no one to bother me."

Thus, Edward ended his pit stop with me. He had spent his life trying to survive a vicious external world and trying to find his way through a vicious internal world. He survived but at a great price. His pit stop was not voluntary. Perhaps his next one will be of his own choice. Edward's struggle with feeling persecuted by the world was in part the result of his primitive depressive guilt and anxiety over separating and turning away from what he saw as the incredible needs of his job and his mother. He wanted to take care of himself for a change but didn't want to abandon his job/mother for fear of causing hurt and hate.

For a bit, I fell into his defenses against these anxieties by interpreting his sense of burden and guilt, rather than interpreting his desire and fear of differentiation, growth, and change. Both interpretive directions were accurate, but the first was more of a collusion with his projected defenses against intense paranoid and depressive phantasies and the second was more his core conflict and desire.

SUMMARY

Hinshelwood (2003) has noted that the Kleinian understanding of counter-transference and the Kleinian technical approach has been greatly influenced by Bion's (1959) concept of containment. Hinshelwood outlines the three possible outcomes in that process. In the first level, the analyst/mother reacts to the intensity or forbidden nature of the patient's projections by becoming rigid or unaccepting, causing the projection and the patient's internal experiences to become formless, meaningless, or unprotected. Bion (1959) has explained how the analyst/mother needs to be to a degree disturbed in order to be able to acknowledge the disturbance in the patient, but not so disturbed as to reject the patient's anxiety or desire.

The second level of containment is the more ideal result. The analyst/mother becomes a flexible, accepting container who is affected by the projections but only in a way that is beneficial to both parties. Initially, the analyst does feel the dread, guilt, persecution, and confusion in unison with the patient or even in isolation after the projective discharge, but hopefully sustains their greater ability to integrate, understand, and ultimately teach via returning the modified projection through the vehicle of interpretation.

The third possible result of projective identification is when the projection overwhelms the analyst and the container function collapses or becomes fragmented and splintered. Hinshelwood (2003) notes that failure to properly contain is to be expected but an ongoing effort to regain and maintain a mental balance is critical. When the analyst becomes confused or overwhelmed by the projection of the patient's defensive system, he is likely to become rigid, critical, or even soothing in an artificial, carbon copy or echo sort of way that does not really soothe, heal, or support because it is in fact a collusion with the patient against certain taboo ways of thinking, feeling, or acting. These taboo states tend to be focused around individuation, growth, difference, and separation.

Segal (1975) has noted how important it is for the patient to internalize a new object who is capable of containing and transforming their anxiety. I would add that it is vital, especially for the type of patients outlined in the case material who are worried about the implications of their independent, individual strivings, to be able to introject a new version of the object who is not only capable but willing to accept, contain, and transform. I think many of our patients, such as the two outlined in the case material, do not trust that we are willing to take on their hidden desires for change, difference, separation, and challenge so they chose instead to project a variety of defenses that block, cloak, or obscure these wishes and thus protect themselves and the object from possible retribution, injury, loss, or disappointment.

In conclusion, there are times when the patient's over reliance on projective identification brings both patient and analyst into a mutual defensive position that feels comfortable and repetitive. This pattern of mutual avoidance comes forth in the analyst's ongoing interpretive acting out of certain object relational phantasies that take the focus away from other more conflicted aspects of the patient's internal world. While Kleinians view projective identification as involving elements that can be solely within the patient's unconscious phantasy world, they also have delineated ways in which projective identification becomes part of the interpersonal and interactional situation by which both patient and analyst act out various projected roles.

This paper has described how counter-transference acting out can cause the analyst to interpret only selective aspects of the patient's desires or fears and avoids or denies others, thus colluding with the patient's basic defenses against these uncomfortable states of mind. The analyst process and the successful establishment of analyst contact (Waska 2007), create the potential space for new knowledge and understanding which can create dependence and union as well as independence and separation between internal links of self and other. This potential psychological change can be extremely threatening in the mind of the patient, who is filled with paranoid-schizoid and/or depressive anxieties for self and object. Therefore, to eliminate this intolerable and unbearable state, the patient may resort to intense projective identification in which he draws the analyst into a mutual defensive acting out. The analyst's part in this unfolds in a series of one-sided interpretations (Feldman 1991)

If the analyst is in fact made guilty, anxious, or angry by the patient's projection of separateness, difference, and division, he may be more susceptible to enacting a common or mutual defensive posture against them. The analyst can escape his own embarrassment, shame, or judgment by ignoring, denying, or camouflaging his reactions and turning to another focus instead. This becomes a transference/counter-transference union in flight against certain other elements of the patient that were split off with projective identification. The mutual defense reassures both parties, at least temporarily, that all is ok and that the object is not angry, destroyed, or lost.

Joseph (1988;1989), O'shaughnessy (1992), and Carpy (1989) have all pointed out that enactments, including the interpretive variety examined in this paper, are inevitable, but if properly handled can provide valuable clinical information about the patient's struggles with self and object. Once the analyst recovers his analytic balance, he can find the freedom to allow the patient to be different in his own mind. This provides a new type of object for the patient to introject, one that accepts and allows new, different, and separate ways of thinking and feeling that can exist without damage to or attack from self and/or other.

Of course, this will feel refreshing, relieving, and supportive to the patient but also alarming, unfamiliar, and alien. Therefore, the initial anxiety and mistrust of this new object can provoke yet another cycle of defensive projective identification that is pushed into the analyst for aggressive, protective, and reparative reasons. Once again the analyst will need to work through the paranoid and depressive counter-transference reactions to this, especially as they affect the interpretive arena. The consistent working through of this cycle is necessary in the overall healing and transformation the psychoanalytic process can provide patients.

REFERENCES

Bion, W. (1959). Attacks on Linking. *International Journal of Psycho-Analysis* *40*, 308-315.

Carpy, D. (1989). Tolerating the Counter-Transference, *International Journal of Psychoanalysis*, 287-294.

Elmhirst, S. (1978). Time and the Pre-Verbal Transference. *International Journal of Psycho-Analysis, 59*, 173-180.

Feldman, M. (1991). Projective Identification: The Analyst's Involvement, *International Journal of Psychoanalysis, 78,* 227.

Heimann, P. (1950). On Counter-Transference. *International Journal of Psycho-Analysis, 31,* 81-84.

Hinshelwood, R. (2003). Counter-Transference and the Therapeutic Relationship: *Recent Kleinian Developments in Technique,* Psyche Matters.com.

Joseph, B. (1985). Transference: The Total Situation. *International Journal of Psycho-Analysis, 66,* 447-454.

Joseph, B. (1988). Object Relations in Clinical Practice, *Psychoanalytic Quarterly, 57,* 626-642.

Joseph, B. (1989). *Psychic Equilibrium and Psychic Change,* Routledge, London.

Klein, M. (1935). A Contribution to the Psychogenesis of Manic-Depressive States. *International Journal of Psycho-Analysis, 16,* 145-174.

Klein, M. (1940). Mourning and its Relation to Manic-Depressive States. *International Journal of Psycho-Analysis, 21,* 125-153.

Klein, M. (1946). Notes on Some Schizoid Mechanisms. *International Journal of Psycho-Analysis, 27,* 99-110.

Money-Kyrle, R. (1956). Normal Counter-Transference and Some of its Deviations. *International Journal of Psycho-Analysis, 37,* 360-366.

O'Shaughnessy, E. (1992). Enclaves and Excursions, *International Journal of Psychoanalysis, 73,* 603-611.

Segal, H. (1975). *A Psychoanalytic Approach to the Treatment of Schizophrenia, in Studies in Schizophrenia,* edited by Malcolm Lader; Ashford, Headly.

In: Psychology of Hate
Editors: Carol T. Lockhardt, pp.121-135

ISBN: 978-1-61668-050-3
© 2010 Nova Science Publishers, Inc.

Chapter 6

HATE AND LOVE SCRIPTS – COMMON ELEMENTS

Barbara Gawda

Department of Psychology, Maria Curie-Sklodowska University,
Lublin, Poland

ABSTRACT

The presented research explains the common traits of affective scripts of hate and love and examines their mysterious nearness. We propose that this nearness is connected to common elements of mental representations of these feelings. The text first describes the script conceptions, the scripts theories concerning love and hate, and the theories that explain their nearness. The authors analyzed 180 stories about love and 180 stories about hate from the same group of people. These participants were of the same age, intellect, and educational level. The aspects of content and structure of scripts were compared. We concentrated on Schank and Abelson's conception of script elements: partner (positive/negative characteristics and emotions), actions (away from others/towards others), actor (positive/negative emotions), and story's type of ending (positive/negative). We used a multidimensional scaling method, Proxscal, to show the two scripts' common area.

INTRODUCTION

According to cognitive psychology, especially cognitive constructivism, emotions and feelings are special cognitive constructs that are coded as representations. Representations are constructed by various types of codes, such as verbal, perceptive, and abstractive (Maruszewski & Scigała, 1998). Verbal representations contain vocabulary and notions; perceptive representations contain images and visions; abstractive representations contain symbols and metaphors. All these representations are organized hierarchically in the mind. The most general representations are metaschemata, which contain information about many schemata and scripts. Schemata are less general than metaschemata; they contain information about phenomena, such as the schemata of romantic love. The least general scripts are constructed by multiple repetitions of a sequence of social events (Rumelhart, 1980). According to Schank and Abelson's (1977) theory, each script is composed of special elements: sequence of scenes (activities), actors, props, causes of scene, and results.

An affective script is a form of the cognitive representation of the sequence of events that have affective meaning. This script is a way of understanding and interpreting the affective situation (Tomkins, 1987; Demorest & Alexander, 1992). After examining the relevant literature, we can conclude that the scripts are the elements of schemata. For example, the schemata of romantic love contain several scripts, such as scripts of dating, scripts of overcoming obstacles, scripts of breaking up, etc. These scripts are probably organized in a hierarchy that is focused on the main subject (Tomkins, 1987; Berne, 2005; White, 2005). The affective scripts can be more or less general, according to Sternberg's (1998) theory. Sternberg describes various types of love scripts: detailed scenarios of dates, and social situations like parties, meeting with friends, etc.

Our research focused on love and hate scripts. Scientists have discussed the different types of love relationships and the several stages of those relationships (Beall & Sternberg, 1995; Choo et al., 1993; Wojciszke, 2003). According to the literature, love can be defined as a feeling, a symbol, and a value. As a symbol, this most durable element of human culture has existed throughout all historical ages and political systems. As a value, according to some philosophical theories, love has great importance in a single person's life and in society as a whole. Love is the ideal form of a social relationship.

Eibl-Eibesfeldt (1995) suggests that people are naturally programmed to feel positive emotions such as love. Love significantly influences the development of people's social capacities and defense mechanisms (Davis & Latty-Mann, 1987). The diversity of love-related experiences is caused by many factors, such as sex, age, personality, temperamental traits, and emotional maturity (Hendrick & Hendrick, 1986; Sternberg, 1988; Sternberg, 1998).

This study examines the feeling of love in relationships between heterosexual partners. In this context, love is defined as a strong, complex emotion that has a positive valence. Love can contain happiness, joy, and euphoria, as well as sadness, anxiety, or shame (Lee, 1973).

Hate is also a strong, complex, affective emotion, but it has a negative valence; it is a feeling of repulsion. It can contain disgust, anger, contempt, and rage (Zaleski, 1998). Sometimes, hate is a form of vengeance; instead of seeking revenge, a person can simply hate the object of his or her displeasure (Lewis & Haviland-Jones, 2000). Hate regulates relationships between people by separating two persons who hate each other. In some sense, a feeling of hate supports subjective well-being. Hate protects a person's self. In some situations, however, this protection could be cruel. Moreover, one's subjective well-being is not fulfilled by hating because remorse can follow it.

The literature presents various opinions about the special nearness of love and hate. Wojciszke (2003) notes, "The dramatic nearness of love and hate is a popular main topic of many works from classical tragedy to nowadays" (p. 131). Many researchers have tried to explain this "mysterious" nearness. On the basis of Freud's theory of the "narcissism of small differences," some psychoanalysts think that love always contains hate; i.e., hate is an element of love. These common elements develop between partners because each person needs to be with somebody but simultaneously needs to be different and separated from that partner (Gabbard, 1993).

According to Freud's conception of the instinctive nature of human beings, the opposing feelings of love and hate come from two opposite instincts, Eros and Thanatos. Eros concerns positive feelings and emotions, whereas Thanatos contains negative and destructive emotions. These two instincts cause different types of behavior, provoking the strong and opposite feelings of love and hate. This theory does not explain how a strong positive feeling changes into a strong negative feeling.

The second possible explanation for the mechanism of transforming love into hate is Solomon's (1980) theory of the opponent process. Solomon proposed an opponent process theory to account for motivational and affective dynamics. This theory asserts that the brain avoids extremes of emotional experience by countering the stimulation it receives with an opposite or "opponent" reaction. Opponent processes are thought to be responsible for the characteristic changes in affective experience that occur over time; hence, they account for the dynamics of affective response. This theory explains that two opposite feelings, such as love and hate, can easily be evoked at the same time.

Such an easy transformation from love to hate is related to the specificity of strong emotions. Both positive strong feelings and negative strong feelings cause after-effects that have opponent valences. The love after-effect has a negative valence, but the hate after-effect has a positive valence. The negative after-effect of love is stronger because all negative emotions and feelings have longer duration. Because of its longer duration, the negative love after-effect could have more influence on human behavior and on the quality of relationships that are based on love.

Neurophysiological theories provide the third possible explanation of the mysterious nearness of love and hate. MacLean (1993) suggests that the nearness of love and hate could be explained by the anatomical and neurochemical basis for mechanisms of reward and aversion, especially in the connections between the neural structures. The award system in the brain is connected to the aversive system. Studies have shown that brain reward and aversive systems are based on multiple neural elements. Strong stimulation of one structure evokes the stimulation of another structure. The effect of this strong stimulation could appear as opponent feelings and emotions.

Considering the theoretical background, we hypothesize that the "mysterious" nearness originates from the affective representation of two opponent feelings. We suggest that this nearness is connected to the similarities of love and hate scripts. These two feelings develop together, and their mental representations are constructed together over time. The neurophysiological mechanisms create a basis for two opponent feelings. Therefore, the love and hate schemata could have a significant area in common. That is why love can be easily transformed into hate and hate into love.

This thesis is based on data about the schemata's functions. The schemata are responsible for formulating thoughts and opinions, coding information, forming perceptions, and controlling emotional reactions to a stimulus (Weyr & Srull, 1986). The schemata and the scripts are related to complex affectivity because the affectivity is influenced not only by the physiological component of an emotional reaction but also, even primarily, by the cognitive component. Scherer (2000) notes that "a feeling" refers to a complex and usually strong subjective human response (i.e., a complex emotion). A complex emotion such as love or hate contains several components: cognitive appraisal processes, intraorganismic adaptation and regulation of somato-visceral systems, motor expression, action tendencies, and subjective feelings (Scherer, 2000). This cognitive component of two feelings (love and hate) is the subject of our study.

The monological narrative discourse was used as an investigation method because the narration is treated as a means of comprehending the mental schema. We expect that in the narrations, some elements of affective scripts (love scripts) will be expressed. That is why two opposite situations were presented in the photos: a date and a quarrel. Our supposition was based on narrative theories, which consider narration to be a means of cognitive representation of reality; i.e., it reflects the way people understand the world (Bruner, 1991; McAdams, 1993; Sarbin 1995; Sternberg, 1998).

This way of investigating scripts is based on as the strategies set forth by Tomkins (1987), Demorest and Alexander (1992), and Wierzbicka (1992). Narratives are treated as structures that reflect one's perception of the world (Sarbin, 1989; Trzebiński, 2002).

As a consequence of the adopted theoretical background, the following research question was formulated. Are there any common elements among the love and hate scripts expressed in the narratives? This study attempts to answer that question by testing the following hypothesis. We expect that love and hate scripts contain similar elements or common aspects. It is impossible to specify a hypothesis about the character of these elements because no literature has addressed that topic.

METHOD

Participants

Participants were sampled from a group of students who attended extramural or evening secondary schools. The research program was advertised in those schools. Participants voluntarily answered the announcement. They were not paid. The study covered a group of adult subjects who had working-class backgrounds. The data selected for the final analysis were based on 180 persons (90 men and 90 women) in the age range of 21 to 46 years (M = 33.5; SD = 12.5). The subjects had all received similar educations (elementary vocational schools), and all were of average intellectual capacity (WAIS-R: M = 99, SD = 6.5; verbal intelligence: IQ = 93 - 105). Primary interviews excluded subjects with higher-than-average educational achievements (particularly in Polish language classes) as well as those with apparent educational difficulties ($N = 30$).

Procedure

Two photographs were chosen from the sixteen (eight for love and eight for hate) that were used during the pilot study. A voluntary sample of 40 persons (20 men, 20 women; of differential education levels) was asked to look at the photographs, which were shown individually, to describe what happened in the situation presented in each picture, and to explain what kind of feeling they identified in the picture and whether they recognized the feeling as love or as hate. They rated the photographs for each emotion on a 3-point scale (1 – "slightly agree"; 2 "agree at some point"; 3 "strongly agree"). After that, their responses were compared and a test of inter-rater agreement between their judgments was conducted. The photograph that received the most significant value (love: W-Kendall test = 0.93; hate: W-Kendall test = 0.86) was chosen for the following stage of the investigation.

Following the comprehensive interviews and background data-gathering, the research subjects were given single sheets of paper along with two photographs chosen from the pilot study, one of a couple hugging each other, and one of a contemptuous couple quarreling with each other. They were asked to participate in this investigation concerning the opinions and interests of adults, and they received the following instructions: "Look at the picture. Imagine that you are one of the people in the photograph. Try to identify with his or her role. Write a story about your role." The participants did not know the purpose of the investigation. They had been informed about anonymous participation in the study. Each of the participants wrote a story about the perceived love and a story about the perceived hate. We then examined the resulting 180 stories about love and 180 stories about hate.

Scripts Analysis

In sum, we analyzed 360 stories in terms of typical script elements, according to the literature. The aspects of the structure and content of the scripts were taken from Schank and Abelson (1977) as well as from the works of Gawda (2008a, 2008b), Tomkins (1987), and Wierzbicka (1992). The frequent aspects of the scripts were causes of the situation, actors, actions, place, time, props, and ending of the scene. The typology proposed by Sternberg (1998) contains several different forms of scripts: asymmetrical (about teacher and student), about objects, symmetrical, narrative. Therefore, the actors in the script could be described as positive or negative, as could the ending of the scene. The scenes included many different types of actions. We choose some typical elements of the scripts:

Description of partner (wife, husband, boyfriend, girlfriend, named, women, man): positive (i.e., "She is good") or negative (i.e., "She is awful").

Actions away from others (i.e., "I would escape") and actions towards others (i.e., "I want touch you").

Emotions of actor: positive (i.e., "I am happy") or negative (i.e., "I am not happy").

Emotions of partner: positive (i.e., "my wife is very happy"), negative (i.e., "my wife is unhappy").

Type of the ending of the story: positive (i.e., "everything will be OK") or negative (i.e., "I feel it is not for me").

Three examiners assessed the indicators in the stories independently. Next, the scores were averaged for each participant. The examiners were in 96% agreement.

RESULTS

The descriptions of the partners were analyzed. The partners were termed as wife and husband, woman and man, boyfriend and girlfriend, named persons, or named by pronouns (i.e., he and she) in both types of stories. The narratives about hate were more often about spouses, whereas the stories about love more often concerned persons outside of marriage, i.e., "my boyfriend," "my girlfriend." A similar number of actors and partners were called "this woman" or "this man." The stories about hate contained more pronouns than the love stories.

The descriptions of partners were mostly positive in the stories about love and more often negative in the stories about hate. The partners' characteristics presented in the love stories were "wonderful," "good," "fantastic," "amazing," "the best," "the most beautiful," "excellent," etc. Sometimes, in the stories about love, partners were suspected of insincere intentions, short vision, or not considering of all consequences of their behaviors. The negative characteristics presented in the stories about hate were descriptions like "hopeless," "awful," "horrible," "bestial," "malicious," "lazy," "cretin," "insincere," and "dishonest." In these narratives, positive descriptions of the partners sometimes appeared: "In sum he is good, valuable, but I cannot forgive him for what he has done." "He is able to be warm. "So far away she was good and understanding, but now she is awful."

The actions were defined as concrete activities and also as behavior; this was mostly indicated by verbs, i.e. "to touch," "to avoid," "to give." We discerned the actions that were towards others, such as "to touch somebody," "to give the flowers." Other actions were away from the others, such as "to turn one's back," "to avoid," "to go away," "to leave somebody."

There were more actions towards other people and fewer actions away from them in the stories about love. In the love stories, the actors and partners tried to form or support their relationships, endeavoring to be close to each other, but sometimes they felt anxious or jealous and hence presented actions away from the others.

Conversely, in the stories about hate, there were more actions away from others, such as "turning one's back," "leaving," "going out," "rejecting," "throwing," "pushing back," and "manifesting a dislike." We can conclude that both love and hate scripts contain actions both toward and away from the other people but that love scripts present more actions towards, whereas hate scripts present more actions away from others.

We analyzed the types of endings of the hate stories and the love stories. Not every story was finished by an ending; several stories lacked any specific conclusion. In general, the narratives about love were finished by positive endings (i.e., "everything will be well"), but some of them were concluded by negative endings (i.e., "somebody is afraid and prefers not to continue this relationship in order to avoid engagement"). A few stories about hate ended positively (i.e., "to calm somebody"), but the majority of them ended negatively (i.e., "to throw his clothes on street and reject him"). The negative endings of love scripts were connected to anxiety that "soon our happiness will be over," whereas the negative endings of hate scripts were related to predictions that "soon it happen something bad, wrong" or that "it looks bad."

A multidimensional scaling Proxscal was conducted to compare the love and hate scripts. We conducted an analysis of three aspects: descriptions of partners in love and hate scripts, actions in hate and love scripts, and types of endings in love and hate scripts. The Proxscal analysis shows two dimensions. First, there is a large cluster composed of negative descriptions of partners in the love stories, positive perceptions of partners in the hate stories, actions toward partners in love stories, and actions away from partners in both love and hate narratives.

Table 1. Descriptive Statistics

Script's elements	Love M	Love SD	Hate M	Hate SD
Partner positive	3.04	1.19	1.09	0.23
Partner negative	0.88	0.48	4.50	1.81
Actions from	1.72	0.57	4.14	1.60
Actions towards	4.48	2.81	1.12	0.92
Emotions actor positive	7.8	5.3	1.4	1.0
Emotions actor negative	0.9	0.32	3.4	1.9
Emotions partner positive	5.6	3.6	0.8	0.56
Emotions partner negative	1.2	0.9	6.8	4.6
Ending of story – positive	0.86	0.45	0.18	0.1
Ending of story – negative	0.1	0.08	0.75	0.23

Some elements of love scripts are related to some aspects of hate scripts. Probably, an ambivalence or anxiety is the main factor that connects all these elements of the two script types. This feeling hinders people from discerning the border between positive and negative feelings. In this cluster, the actions away from the others in love scripts and in hate scripts are closely related. In both situations, the actions away from partners have the same goal—avoiding—and that goal is determined by fear. Anxiety probably plays similar roles in both scripts.

Some clusters are independent from the other aspects. The negative descriptions of partners in hate stories are related to the hate narratives' negative endings. It is probable that such characteristics concern extremely negative behavior, which is specific to the hate situation. The logical consequence of a negative partner description is a negative ending.

The Proxscal analysis shows a second dimension; the negative endings of love scripts are completely unrelated to other elements of scripts. This type of ending may be caused by anxiety or by special circumstances.

Interestingly, two variables form an independent cluster; the positive endings of love stories closely related to positive descriptions of partners in the love scripts. This type of ending is typical to love and is determined by clear emotional states such as happiness and pleasure; hence, there is no relation between it and other aspects. The same conclusion probably applies to positive descriptions of partners in love scripts. A positive perception is essential to and evident in the feeling of love; hence, it could be unrelated to other states.

Object Points

Common Space

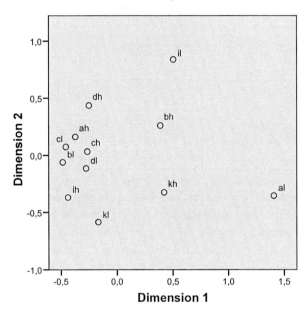

Indicators of variables:

al (positive description of partner in love), ah (positive description of partner in hate),

bl (negative description of partner in love), bh (negative description of partner in hate),

cl (actions from in love), ch (actions from in hate),

dl (actions towards in love), dh (actions towards in hate),

il (positive endings of the stories about love), ih (positive endings of the stories about hate),

kl (negative endings of stories about love), kh (negative endings of stories about hate)

Normalized Raw Stress	,03239
Stress-I	,17996(a)
Stress-II	,35091(a)
S-Stress	,07459(b)
Tucker's Coefficient of Congruence	,98367

Figure 1. Love and hate scripts: Valence of description of partner, actions from away and towards, endings of stories (Proxscal analysis)

Object Points

Common Space

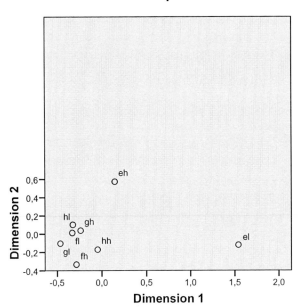

Indicators of variables:
el (positive actor's emotions in love), eh (positive actor's emotions in hate),
fl (negative actor's emotions in love), fh (negative actor's emotions in hate),
gl (positive partner's emotions in love), gh (positive partner's emotions in hate),
hl (negative partner's emotions in love), hh (negative partner's emotions in hate),

Normalized Raw Stress	,00861
Stress-I	,09277(a)
Stress-II	,14496(a)
S-Stress	,01637(b)
Tucker's Coefficient of Congruence	,99569

Figure 2. Love and hate scripts – valence of actor's and partner's emotions (Proxscal scaling)

   The actions toward others in the hate scripts are related to the positive descriptions of partners in hate stories. These actions are probably focused on resolving problems, understanding the partner's behavior, and finding a solution.

A positive description of a partner in a hate story indicates hope and cooperative activities.

The second step of the analysis concerned the dimensions of positive and negative emotional states of the primary actors and their partners. A Proxscal analysis was executed to find similarities and differences between the actor's and the partner's emotions in both hate and love stories. In general, love is a complex feeling that includes more positive than negative emotions, whereas hate is an opponent feeling (Hatfield & Rapson, 1996). Typical emotions presented in love scripts are happiness, ecstasy, joy, pleasure, satisfaction, fulfillment, passion, euphoria, delight, adoration, and excitement. Sometimes, the actors or partners in the love scripts feel negative emotions such as anxiety, jealousy, and fear.

Typical descriptions of emotional states in hate scripts are negative. Actors and partners feel anger, sadness, hate, rage, aversion, envy, emotional injury, contempt, helplessness, and dislike. The hate scripts also contain some positive emotions; the actors and partners experience positive thoughts, such as "... at last he has gone away, I am calm," and "I feel relief."

The scaling analysis shows the relations between positive emotions of the actors in love and hate scripts. The actor's positive perspective is unrelated to other script elements, and the positive states in both scripts are similar. Positive emotions of actors in love and hate scripts are independent of other emotions. From the actor's perspective, the description of the actor's emotions is different from the partner's emotions because the actor describes himself.

A significant cluster comprises the actors' negative emotions in both love and hate scripts as well the negative and positive emotions of the partners in both love and hate situations. All emotions are very close. Perhaps persons who tend to express negative emotions possess better capacities for recognizing both negative and positive states in their partners' behavior. There is a difference between the two perspectives of perception. The first entails recognizing one's own positive emotions and describing one's partner's; the second includes perceiving one's own negative emotional state and describing one's partner's. Most likely, these two points of view are independent.

CONCLUSION

The comparison of love and hate scripts reveals both differences and similarities. The positive elements in hate scripts are related to love scripts. The negative elements in love scripts are similar to hate scripts. We conclude that there is a common area for the two scripts. Interestingly, we find that some elements in both scripts are unrelated to other aspects. The elements typical to hate scripts are negative descriptions of partners and negative endings. The typical aspects of love situations are positive descriptions of partners and positive endings. This suggests that there is a common area for love and hate scripts as well as separate areas typical for each different type of script. This proves the prototypical construction of scripts (Cantor & Mischel, 1977). Both scripts have prototypical elements and areas of possible transformation, according to Fehr (2005). The area of possible transformation could be related to another script. The borders of complex emotions such as love and hate may be imprecise. Most likely, these two scripts develop together over time. In love scripts, relationships are less formal than in hate scripts. That means that hate is the result of accumulating a greater number of negative experiences. The forming of hate script requires more time (Zaleski, 1998).

A love script can be activated while a positive evaluation of partner is accessible; this sets in motion several positive states. A hate script is activated when a negative evaluation of one's partner is available. In both types of scripts, many actions attempt to establish and support relationships. Hate scripts contain more actions focused on rejection, disagreement, or disapproval, which are effects of negative emotional states. Both types of scripts contain the same types of actors and partners; their circumstances are similar, and they execute similar actions. The situations differ by valence of emotional states and evaluations of persons.

REFERENCES

Beall, A. E. & Sternberg, R. (1995). The social construction of Love, *Journal of Social and Personal relationships, 12*, 417-438.

Berne, E. (2005). *Dzień dobry...i co dalej?* Poznań: Dom Wydawniczy Rebis. (*What do you say after say hello?*).

Bruner, J. S. (1991). The narrative construction of reality. *Critical Inquiry, 18*, 1-21.

Cantor, N. & Mischel, W. (1977). Traits as prototypes: Effects on recognition memory, *Journal of Personality and Social Psychology, 35*, 38 - 48.

Choo, P., Levine, T. & Hatfield, E. (1996). Gender, love schemas, and reactions to romantic break-ups. *Journal of Social Behavior and Personality, 11*, 143-160.

Davis, K. E. & Latty-Mann, H. (1987). Love style and relationship quality: A contribution to validation. *Journal of Social and Personal Relationships, 4,* 409-428.

Demorest, A. P. & Alexander, I. E. (1992). Affective scripts as organizers of personal experience. *Journal of Personality, 60,* 645-663.

Eibl-Eibesfeldt, I. (1995). *Miłość i nienawiść.* Warszawa: PWN. (*Love and hate*).

Fehr, B. (2005). The role of Prototype in interpersonal cognition. In M. W. Baldwin (Eds.) *Interpersonal Cognition* (180-206). New York, London: Guilford Press.

Freud, S. (1992/1917). *Wstęp do psychoanalizy.* Warszawa: PWN. (*Introduction to psychoanalysis*).

Gabbard, G. (1993). On hate in love relationships: The narcissism of minor differences revised. *Psychoanalytic Quarterly, 62,* 229-238.

Gawda, B. (2008a). Gender differences in verbal expression of love schema. *Sex Roles: Journal of Research. 58,* 814-821.

Gawda, B. (2008b). Love scripts of persons with antisocial personality. *Psychological Reports, 103,* 371-380.

Hatfield, E. & Rapson, R. L. (1996). *Love and sex: Cross-cultural perspectives.* Needham Heights, MA: Allyn & Bacon.

Hendrick, C. & Hendrick, S. S. (1986). A theory and method of love. *Journal of Personality and Social Psychology, 50,* 392-402.

Lee, J. A. (1973). *The colors of love: An exploration of the ways of loving.* Don Mills: New Press.

Lewis, M. & Haviland-Jones, J. (2000). *Handbook of emotions.* New York, London: Guilford Press.

MacLean, P. D. (1993). Cerebral evolution of emotion. In M. Lewis, & J. M. Haviland (Eds.) *Handbook of emotions* (67-83). New York, London: Guilford Press.

Maruszewski, T. & Ścigała, E. (1998). *Emocje – Aleksytymia – Poznanie.* Poznań: Wydawnictwo Fundacji Humaniora (Emotions – Alexytymie – Cognition).

McAdams, D. P. (1993). *Stories We Live By.* New York: Morrow.

Rumelhart, D. E. (1980). Schemata: The building blocks of cognition. In R. Spiro, B. Bruce & W. Brewer (Eds.) *Theoretical issues in reading comprehension* (33-58). Hillsdale, NJ: Lawrence Erlbaum.

Sarbin, T. (1989). Emotions as narrative employments. In J. Packer & R. Addison (Eds.) *Entering the circle: Hermeneutic investigation in psychology* (185-201). New York: SUNY Press.

Sarbin, T. (1995). Emotional life, rhetoric and roles. *Journal of Narrative and Life History, 5,* 38-50.

Schank, R. C. & Abelson, R. P. (1977). *Scripts, plans, goals and understanding: An inquiry into human knowledge structures.* Oxford: Lawrence Erlbaum.

Scherer, K. R. (2000). Psychological models of emotion. In J. Borod (Eds.) *The neuropsychology of emotion* (137-162). Oxford/New York: Oxford University Press.

Solomon, R. J. (1980). The opponent process theory of acquired motivation. The costs of pleasure and the benefits of pain. *American Psychologist, 35*, 691-712.

Sternberg, R. J. (1988). *The triangle of love.* New York: Basic Books.

Sternberg, R. J. (1998). *Love is a story.* Oxford: Oxford University Press.

Tomkins, S. S. (1987). Script theory. In J. Aronoff, A. Robin, & R. Zucker (Eds.) *The emergence of personality* (147-216). New York: Springer.

Trzebiński, J. (1995). Narrative self, understanding, and action. In A. Oesterwegel & R. Wicklund (Eds.) *The self in European and North American culture: Development and process* (73-89). London: Klüver Academic Publishers.

Weyr, R. S. & Srull, T. K. (1986). Human cognition in its social context, *Psychological Review, 93*, 322-359.

White, G. M. (2005). Reprezentacje znaczenia emocjonalnego: kategoria, metafora, schemat, dyskurs. In M. Lewis, & J. M. Haviland-Jones (Eds.) *Psychologia emocji* (53-72). Gdańsk: GWP. (*Psychology of emotions*).

Wierzbicka, A. (1992). *Semantics, culture and cognition.* Oxford: Oxford University Press.

Wojciszke, B. (2003). *Psychologia miłości.* Gdańsk: GWP (*Psychology of love*).

Zaleski, Z. (1998). *Od zawiści do zemsty. Społeczna psychologia kłopotliwych emocji.* Warszawa: Żak. (*From envy to vengeance: Social psychology of difficult emotions*).

In: Psychology of Hate
Editors: Carol T. Lockhardt, pp.137-158 © 2010 Nova Science Publishers, Inc.

ISBN: 978-1-61668-050-3

Chapter 7

HATE: NO CHOICE AGENT SIMULATIONS

Krzysztof Kulakowski, Malgorzata J. Krawczyk
*and Przemyslaw Gawroński**
Faculty of Physics and Applied Computer Science, AGH
University of Science and Technology, al. Mickiewicza 30,
PL-30059 Kraków, Poland

Abstract

We report our recent simulations on the social processes which – in our opinion – lie at the bottom of hate. First simulation deals with the so-called Heider balance where initial purely random preferences split the community into two mutually hostile groups. Second simulation shows that once these groups are formed, the cooperation between them is going to fail. Third simulation provides a numerical illustration of the process of biased learning; the model indicates that lack of objective information is a barrier to new information. Fourth simulation shows that in the presence of a strong conflict between communities hate is unavoidable.

1. Introduction

To write that hate as a subject on a physicist's desk is a challenge is an understatement. For obvious reasons, we are not able to comment what has been

---

*Email address: kulakowski@novell.ftj.agh.edu.pl

written on hate only recently by philosophers, psychologists, sociologists and historians. Still, having in mind what we can deduce about hate from our computer simulations, we feel that it is at least more honest and clear to confess how we imagine the role of the simulation itself in this kind of research.

The simulation is the part of research most safe. Not a surprise, that in various sociophysical papers we the readers are fed with computational details. The devil is before and after; in the model assumptions and in the interpretation of the results. We the authors are somewhat conscious of these dangers, but this knowledge is even not necessary to do what we actually do. Actually in most cases we meet the problems with silence. If, then, our simulations could be of interest for sociologically oriented readers, the reality described by means of these simulations must be simple – this is a necessary condition. As a rule, the input of the model contains some numbers even if their measurement is dubious; a computational model is always expressed with numbers and we are forced to imagine that data are accessible in this or that way. The output – the results of the simulation – should be detectable qualitatively; only then we are able to compare with reality at least the existence of effects obtained in our computers. Summarizing, a typical result of the simulation is that in these and these conditions some effect does appear. We the authors like to think that we simulate some kind of a deterministic machine, the action of which is described with "social" variables. This kind of understanding is not far from what can be found in sociological textbooks. "A social mechanism (...) is a constellation of entities and activities that are linked to one another in such a way that they regularly bring about a particular type of outcome" (Hedström, 2005, p. 11).

"Humans are not numbers." Wrong; we just don't want to be treated as numbers - this statement comes from a famous sociophysicist (Stauffer, 2003), as a mark of old discussion about the unique character of human being in Nature. One of consequences of a possible consensus in this matter would be to decide to what extent the character of laws in social sciences is the same as in physics. While such a conclusion seems to be far, it seems appropriate to specify at least approximately the conditions, when we expect that human behaviour is to some extent deterministic. In our opinion, this is possible when the exceptional character of external circumstances meets standard individuals, who can be represented – for the purposes of the simulation - by numbers. We do not expect that these individuals show any outstanding intelligence, knowledge or heroism. If me meet them on street, we are not more impressed, than some other time with other people. On the contrary, the demand of an external situation should hit basic human needs, as physiological needs, needs of safety or of belongingness (Maslow, 1950). In these conditions we can expect that individual characteristics of people becomes less important; what we learnt in our lives seems to be not applicable. These rare situations provide fuel for wide spectrum of social simulations, from the theory of rational choice (von Neumann and Morgenstern, 1944; Szabó and Fáth, 2008) to human bodies as moving particles under some social forces (Helbing, 1993).

We want to supplement these vague considerations by two remarks. First is the natural position of our field of research between necessity and free will. A subject under full control is out of scientific interest – everything we need is known. On the contrary, a research on subjects which are completely uncontrolled has no vital applications. What is of interest is at the border, where results of research can put forward our abilities. An example of what is at the border in human life is a social norm; after years of efforts some people are able to modify their norms to some extent, while others live and die in the same moral environment. Norms form the sociological context, and human behavior cannot be evaluated in a separation from her or his social norms. Summarizing, in our opinion social norms are at the center of any valuable sociological research. In particular, relation of individuals to hate – whom? – is the subject of a social norm, which can be constitutive for a community.

Second remark is some continuation of what is told above about standard people and non-standard situation. The main handicap of social sciences when compared to physics is the unrepeatability of the measurement. In opinion of at least one coauthor of this text, this difficulty comes more from the context than from the people. People are unique, yes, but this kind of uniqueness is less relevant in situations which we would like to simulate. The point is that it is possible to exchange actors leaving the piece untouched, but not the opposite. If historical events form a pattern, we can talk about a mechanism in the sense of Hedström, which appears more than once. This is rare, but we the researchers must assume that this is possible.

Hate as a socially mediated state of mind overlaps with themes which are well established in socially oriented simulations (Castellano et al, 2009): social norms, cooperation and public opinion. Their common content is a picture of a heterogeneous community, where seemingly unimportant differences can lead to a split into groups. As a consequence, cooperation and contact between members of different groups is deteriorated, mutual understanding is substituted by ignorance, finally the social labeling and hostility emerge between members of different groups. These processes lie at the bottom of hate.

Below we are going to report our recent simulations on these social processes. First simulation described in Section II deals with the so-called Heider balance (Kułakowski, 2007) where initial purely random preferences split the community into two mutually hostile groups. Three subsequent sections describe three other simulations. Second simulation (Kułakowski and Gawroński, 2009) shows that once these groups are formed, the cooperation between them is going to fail. Third simulation (Kulakowski, 2009; Malarz et al, 2009) provides a numerical illustration of the process of biased learning; the model indicates that lack of objective information is a barrier to new informations. Fourth simulation (Kułakowski, 2006) is devoted to the impossibility of cooperation with enemies in the presence of a strong conflict. At the end, there is also some place for conclusions.

2.   Heider Balance

Our story on hate begins from almost nothing. Let us consider personal contacts in some small community. For each two individuals their mutual acceptance depends on intangible details, often imperceptible for others. For some of them this acceptance is better, for some it is worse; if we measure their values with any method, we find that they evolve in time. We can refer to (Murray, 2002) where a method was presented of a measurement of the dynamics of marital interactions. As it was observed in some cases, a mutual exchange of repulsive signals can break off the tie. When such a conflict emerges in front of the community, it influences also the quality of other contacts and so on. Everybody has to decide how the event modified his or her relations with the others. As the arising tensions are often in mutual contradiction, the task is quite complex.

Faced with such contradictory requests, people find however a way to resolve their internal conflicts. Namely, they modify some of their opinions and attitudes in such a way that their coherence is restored. This mechanism was recognized in a series of laboratory experiments by Festinger and other researchers

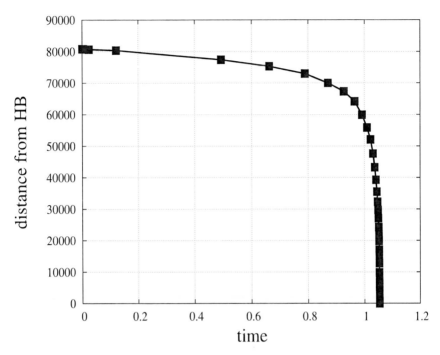

Figure 1: The distance from the state of Heider balance, measured in the number of "negative" triangles, against time.

(Festinger, 1957; Aronson, 1992) and it is known as removing the cognitive dissonance. In this way some negative ties become positive, some positive ones become negative. The final result can be somewhat surprising: the whole community becomes divided into two mutually hostile groups. Still, all the ties within each group are friendly. This state does not evolve any more, because the situation is clear: everybody knows who is enemy and who is friend. Moreover, each friend of other friend is a friend, each enemy of a friend and each friend of an enemy are enemies. This kind of equilibrium is known as the Heider balance (Heider, 1958).

The ideas of the cognitive dissonance and of the Heider balance found an empirical illustration in a controlled psychological experiment by Zachary (Zachary, 1977). For two years, he observed a group of 34 members of a karate club. These observations allowed to construct a friendship networks and to store it in the form of a matrix. Later, a conflict emerged between the administrator of the club and the club's instructor and the group split into two camps (Girvan and Newman, 2002).

Obviously, importance of the work by Zachary for social networks was recognized by sociologists (Hage, 1979; Wasserman and Faust, 1994). As described by Freeman (Freeman, 2008), new impact in sociological applications of the graph theory was given by physicists. Since the publication of the paper of Girvan and Newman (Girvan and Newman, 2002), tens of algorithms have been applied to the Zachary's data. The idea was to check if a given algorithm can reproduce the actual division of the club members.

Now we have to be more specific. The common aim of all these methods was to determine clusters of graph nodes, where nodes are connected more densely within the clusters than between them. A careful reader notices, that the term "more densely" is only qualitative. A mathematically-oriented reader guesses that the task is probabilistic: we set a hypothesis, that clusters do exist, and we extract these clusters from the graph. The actual data may support the hypothesis with some probability. At the end we decide if the obtained probability is large enough. If yes, we accept the obtained cluster structure. Recent reviews on the computational methods of cluster identification can be found in (Fortunato and Castellano, 2009; Fortunato, 2009).

The simulation which we want to underscore here was designed specifically for the problem of the cognitive dissonance. Suppose that each two nodes are connected, what means that every group member has some relations with each other. In the simplest model the links, which represent the friendly or hostile relations between people, are marked with signs: plus or minus, respectively. The cognitive dissonance appears when one negative link makes a triangle with two positive ones, or when three negative links make a triangle. The former case means that two friends of somebody are mutually hostile. The latter is that three individuals are mutually hostile. Lack of cognitive dissonance is then equivalent to a simple condition that the product of three links which make a triangle must be positive. Further, the number of triangles where this product is negative can serve as a quantitative measure of the cognitive dissonance.

The Heider balance attracted attention of several authors – for a review of recent computations see (Kułakowski, 2007). In our calculation (Kułakowski et al, 2005), the links are represented by real numbers $A(i, j)$ between, say, -1 and +1, where i, j are the numbers of nodes. Within this range, their time evolution is governed by the differential equation

$$\frac{dA(i, j)}{dt} = \sum_k A(i, k)A(k, j) \tag{1}$$

In other words, the relation $A(i, j)$ between individuals i and j improves, if most other indviduals k are either friends of both or enemies of both. In these cases, the product $A(i, k)A(k, j)$ is positive. On the contrary, if many individuals k are either enemies of i and friends of j or the opposite, the relation between i and j gets worse: $A(i, j)$ decreases. This is a direct mathematical realization of the removal of the cognitive dissonance. Indeed, the simulation ends in the state without "negative" triangles; this is the state of balance in the Heider sense.

Taking into account the continuous scale of relations allows to observe the character of the time evolution. What is surprising in the obtained data is that the number of the "negative" triangles evolves initially slowly. At a given moment, however, the rate of changes increases very abruptly; an example is presented in Fig. 1. There is yet another interesting result: our Eq. 1 with the Zachary initial data reproduces exactly the division of 34 club members into two groups (Kułakowski et al, 2005).

What we can learn about hate from this simulation is absurdity of its origin. Here we have a real psychological mechanism, namely removing of the cognitive distance. We apply it each day to make our emotional environment more ordered and clear. With this mechanism our hostilities directed towards casual people, formed by occasional events and sometimes irrational thoughts, are transformed into a strong, unambiguous and ordered prejudice against a well defined group. Everybody whom we respect, i.e. each member of our group, confirms that this prejudice is justified. In our group, the group of respected people, this prejudice is a social norm.

What is next?

3.   In-Group Cooperation

In this section we examine one of the currently investigated mechanisms of co-operation, namely the competitive altruism (Roberts, 1998). We show that this mechanism is not immune for the limitation of cooperation to the own player's group. This means, that cooperation does not protect against hate; we can just cooperate with some and hate others.

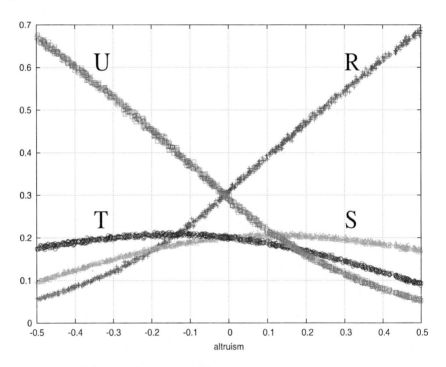

Figure 2: The probability to be in position R, S, T and U against the altruism level e of the player. In particular, the curve R is the probability to cooperate and to meet cooperation. Clearly, this probability increases with the parameter of altruism; when the latter exceeds 0.2, the option R prevails.

The problem of cooperation has been discussed usually in terms of the Pris-oner's Dilemma, abbreviated as PD. In some sense, this dilemma is a challenge for our culture, as it demonstrates its clash with the individual rationality. There is a story which justifies the term PD; as it is commonly known, we prefer another example. Two individuals are imprisoned, and the food is provided between 3.00 AM and 6 AM. A loyal strategy is to get up near, say, 7.00 AM , and to share food evenly. However, the portions are scanty and it is tempting to get up earlier and eat more. The dilemma is to sleep till 7.00 AM or not; once both lie in wait for food, they don't sleep well. In an adopted terminology about PD, to sleep peacefully means "to cooperate", and to lie in wait means "to defect". The amount of situations which could illustrate PD is innumerable, from the Kyoto Protocol back to the biblical story on the Prodigal Son.

Standard representation of PD in game theory is the payoff matrix (Straffin, 1993)

	Cooperate	Defect
Cooperate	R, R	S, T
Defect	T, S	U, U

When a cooperator meets a cooperator, the payoff is R (reward) for both. When both of them defect, both get U (uncooperative). However, once a cooperator meets a defector, the latter gets T (temptation), and the former gets S (sucker's payoff). The game can be classified as PD if $S < U < R < T$. Additional condition is that $T + S < 2R$, to exclude the cyclic strategy when one cooperate and other defects or the opposite. As $R < T$ and $S < U$, to defect is always better than to cooperate; then, according to game theory, a rational player should defect. The point is that if both defect, they get less than if both cooperate.

As we see, PD is designed as to disable cooperation of rational players. Still we can imagine that people cooperate for reasons other than a simple individual profit. These reasons can be kinship and direct or indirect reciprocity; for recent reviews on cooperation theory see for example (Fehr and Fischbacher, 2005). Motivation by kinship is limited to the own group. Motivation by reciprocity can also lead to in-group favoritism, if the group members expect reciprocation from the same group (Fehr and Fischbacher, 2005). Before we switch to the motivation by the competitive altruism, let us quote one social experiment on randomly formed groups.

The aim of this research (Goette et al, 2006) was to check if the mere dependence to a group causes a non-selfish behaviour between its members. The PD experiment with some modifications was conducted in the frames of the Swiss

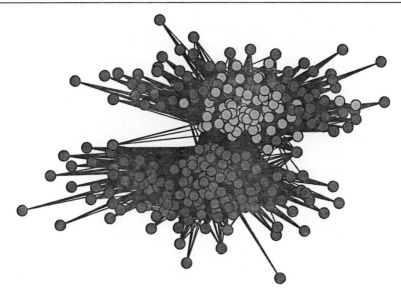

Figure 3: Graph visualization of strong cooperation within two groups, with players with negative altruism left aside; $\kappa = 0.3$

army, where the assignment of individuals to platoons was completely random. Still, after three-weeks training, the cooperation between members of the same platoon was significantly higher, than between members of different platoons. We note that hostility between different platoons has not been observed – fortunately hate does not appear so easily.

We refer to this experiment as it provides a demonstration, that the formation of a group or a community is equivalent to the formation of some social norm, which unifies the group. This equivalence was clearly expressed by a historian, Elias Bickerman: "The first need of any social system is to create incentives to make people do more work than that required by their immediate wants." (Bickerman, 1973, p.73). This means also that expectation of cooperation of members of the same group is stronger. In longer time scale, such an expectation is converted to trust.

The theory of competitive altruism (Roberts, 1998; Van Vugt et al, 2007) explores the cooperation as a demonstration of resources. First assumption is that individuals differ in their level of altruism. Second is that people compete to establish altruistic reputation. In accordance of the Zahavi handicap principle (Zahavi and Zahavi, 1997), the signal must be costful to be reliable. The altruistic behaviour fulfils this condition. Our question is, if this mechanism can be responsible for the group formation, with enhancement of cooperation within groups. Then we could draw a line from the Goette's experiment to the concept of competitive altruism. The problem of hate is left aside till the end of this section.

To address the above question, we resort to a simulation. The model is adopted from our previous work (Kułakowski and Gawroński, 2009); having the paper published we found that its assumptions can be justified within the theory of competitive altruism. These assumptions are:

1. Agents i differ in their altruism level $e(i)$.

2. The probability $P(i, j)$ that an agent i cooperates with another agent j increases with the altruism of i and with the reputation of j. Namely, we used the sum $P(i, j) = e(i) + W(i)$, limited to the range (0,1).

3. The reputation $W(i)$ of i increases when i cooperates, and decreases when i defects.

Most important result of the model is shown in Fig. 2. As we see, the probability that i-th agent meets a cooperative co-player depends on the altruism of i. Most altruistic agents experience cooperation in seventy percent of games. This is true for any payoff we would like to assign to particular outcomes of PD. Then, the values of the payoffs are not relevant.

To investigate the case of two groups, the scheme of simulation was modified (Gawroński et al, 2009) by adding a constant κ to the probability of cooperation if the co-player belongs to the same group; in the opposite case, the same constant κ was subtracted. This modification altered the matrix of the probability of cooperation $P(i, j)$. If the constant κ is large enough, this matrix shows a cluster structure; the method is described in (Krawczyk, 2008). Namely, two clusters could be detected: agents in the same clusters cooperate more frequently, than agents in different clusters. A half of agents is left besides the clusters; still, they are more connected either to one or to the other group. This structure is visualized in Fig. 3.

In this way we made a second step on our path. First was the prejudice. Second is the loss of confidence in members of group or community other, than the agent's own group.

4.   Biased Learning

Third step to hate is the lack of understanding.

At the beginning of Section II the method was remarked of a measurement of dynamics of marital status (Murray, 2001). The method was to distinguish couples of low and high risk level by controlling the signals they send during a conversation. These signals, coded into a special system, were gathered by Gottman and Levenson (Gottman and Levenson, 1992) for 73 couples in 1983. The couples were investigated again in 1987. Among the high risk couples, the percentage of divorced was 19 against 7 in low risk group. Then, the character of conversation allowed to predict the future.

In the case of political differences, the outcome can be even more explicit. Character of anonymous statements about politics in the Internet was investigated by Sobkowicz and Sobkowicz (Sobkowicz and Sobkowicz, 2009). In many cases, comments of internauts could be classified as an exchange of insults, with increasing hostility. The point is more than often, the discussion was dominated by adherents of two major Polish political parties, both Center-Right: PiS and PO. The analysis shown that to be hated by opponents is the desired goal as well as to be admired by supporters. What is the origin of this extreme behaviour? We are going to look for the answer in our third simulation, which deals with the public opinion.

The motivation for the simulation comes from the Zaller theory on the mass opinion (Zaller, 1992). It is based on four ideas: "The first is that citizens vary in their habitual attention to politics and hence in their exposure to political information and argumentation in the media. The second is that people are able to react critically to the arguments they encounter only to the extent that they are knowledgeable about political affairs. The third is that citizens do not typically carry around in their heads fixed attitudes on every issue on which a pollster may happen to inquire; rather, they construct "opinion statements" on the fly as they confront each new issue. The fourth is that, in constructing their opinion statements, people make greatest use of ideas that are, for one reason or another, most immediately salient to them..." (Zaller, 1992).

Keeping – as we believe – the content of these ideas, we reformulated the mathematical scheme of the simulation (Kułakowski, 2009). Further generalization of our formalism (Kułakowski and Gronek, 2009; Malarz et al, 2009) is close to the Deffuant model of public opinion (Deffuant et al, 2000). Therefore we term the formulation as the Zaller-Deffuant model from now on. Its core is as follows. Individuals are the subject of a stream of messages produced by the mass media. An individual is represented by a set of messages which she/he received in the past. Further, a message is represented as a point on the plane of issues. The condition to receive a new message is that its distance from any previously accepted message should be shorter than some critical distance a. This critical distance is a measure of the mental capacity of an individual. Each individual starts at it first message with position selected randomly at the plane of issues. Once a new message appears, it is received or not by an individuals, depending on her/his history. The communication between the individuals is maintained by messages, formulated and sent by the individuals. The position of such a message is determined by a temporal average of the messages received previously by the sender.

The output of the simulation is the distribution of probability p that an opinion formulated by an individual on a given issue is YES. For each individual, this probability can be calculated as

$$p = \frac{\sum_t x_t \Theta(x_t)}{\sum_t |x_t|} \tag{2}$$

where $\Theta(x) = 0$ for $x < 0$, $\Theta(x) = 1$ for $x > 0$, and the sums are performed over messages accepted at time t. In particular, p is equal to unity (YES for sure) if all messages received by the individual are on the positive side of the OY axis. On the contrary, $p = 0$ (NO for sure) if the x-th coordinate of all these messages is negative. The obtained distribution of p is calculated over all individuals.

In the simulation, the system as a whole is the subject of a specific test. The stream of messages from the media is symmetric with respect to the axis OY. Then, the individuals have no more arguments for YES than for NO and the opposite. Smart individuals should recognize this symmetry and their probabilities p should be close to $1/2$. Indeed, if the critical distance a is large enough, the distribution of p has a maximum close to $p = 1/2$. However, for small a the distribution of p shows a bimodal character: two maxima appear, for p close to zero and p close to one (Fig. 4). This means, that small mental capacity leads to extreme opinions (Kułakowski, 2009). In other words, less clever people are more sure of their opinions. This paradoxical result can be seen as a sociological counterpart of the physical concept of the spontaneous symmetry breaking.

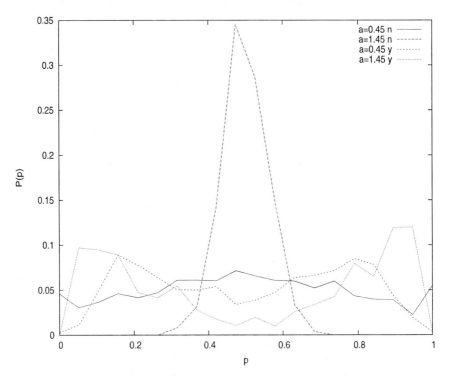

Figure 4: The probability distribution $P(p)$ of the probability p, that an individual opinion about the model issue is YES. Out of four plots, the only one centralized near $p = 0.5$ is the plot for the mental capacity $a = 1.45$, without interaction (marked by n). Other plots are for $a = 0.45$ with and without interaction, and for $a = 1.45$ with interaction (y).

Here we are interested in the consequences of the interpersonal communication. It appears that this form of interaction deteriorates the central maximum of the distribution $P(p)$, as shown also in Fig. 4 (Kułakowski and Gronek, 2009; Malarz et al, 2009). This indicates, that the communication between the group members can maintain prejudice. Such a conclusion coincides with the warnings against the groupthink (Janis, 1972). Even if individuals are endowed with high capacity, the exchange of messages leads to a formation of one single opinion, which is an average over some finite set. The stream of incoming messages is dominated by those exchanged within the system. As a consequence, all individual opinions are the same. The community becomes perfectly homogeneous.

Suppose now that this community contacts with another one, with different opinion. Till this moment, neither mutual understanding nor tolerance was necessary. Individual differences were hidden to maintain the social coherence – now they are exposed and directed against the other group. If hostility appears, we should not be surprised.

5.   Case of Ghetto

To get hate, the last missing ingredient is a spark. It can be imperceptibly small: a discussion between shepherds, a soldier's joke, a tabloid article. Still real wars do not break out like that: real wars are provoked by serious people, who want to be sure of the results of their actions. A good provocation is a murder of a respected person, as Mohandas Ghandi, Martin King, Icchak Rabin. We do not need to discuss an initiation – this is easy. We are interested in the question, if – in the presence of full conflict - the development of hate can be spontaneously halted.

The subject of our last simulation is a ghetto. Historically, the term "ghetto" is ambiguous. Here we use it to describe the situation where the position of people is defined by two traits: i) an attempt of an inhabitant of ghetto to leave the area makes his situation worse, ii) human laws, as understood by inhabitants, are broken by an external power (Kułakowski, 2006). The decision is limited to two strategies: to support the resistance or to obey the rules imposed by the external power. In the psychological dimension, the choice is to hate or not to hate.

In our considerations, we refer to the Maslow theory (Maslow, 1950) remarked at the introduction. According to this theory, we fulfil our needs in a definite order. The physiological needs are most basic and they must be fulfilled at first. Once they are satisfied, we start to bother about safety. Next is the needs for belongingness, esteem and self-actualization, in this order. Our point is that vital decisions of people are biased by their needs. This is in accordance of the fourth postulate of Zaller: "in constructing their opinion statements, people make greatest use of ideas that are, for one reason or another, most immediately salient to them" (Zaller, 1992), quoted in the preceding section. In other words, the decision of resistance and hate is taken in connection of the actual need, yet not satisfied.

Even in a ghetto, people differ in their position and possibilities. There are some, who struggle to satisfy their physiological needs: water and food. These efforts makes their behavior determined and predictable. These people have no opportunity to express their hate – this is too costly. Actually, the simplest way to reduce the resistance of people is to reduce their life to this physiological level. This method is well known and still being applied (Politkovskaya, 2003). There are some other people, who are relatively safe; they can bother about their belongingness, love, friendship and perhaps the higher needs . Their decisions about resistance depend on their individual social entanglements; an attempt to simulate this would be idle. Who remains are the people who concentrate on their safety. Their decision about resistance is connected to this need. Will they be more safe, when obeying the rules of the external power? This is the question most salient for them.

The simulation consists in the numerical solution of the so-called Master equation (van Kampen, 1981)

$$\frac{dr}{dt} = -u(r)r + w(r)(1 - r) \tag{3}$$

where r is the time dependent probability of the choice of resistance and hate, $u(r)$ is the probability of changing the decision from resistance to submission, $w(r)$ is the probability of changing the decision from submission to resistance. What is sought after is the function $r(t)$, while the functions $u(r)$ and $w(r)$ should be given. We note that on the contrary to standard application of this equation in physics of magnetism, $w(r)$ and $u(r)$ are not expected to be equal for $r = 1/2$. The shape of these functions is difficult to be determined, but we can state two details: i) $w(r)$ increases with r, and ii) $u(r)$ decreases with r. These facts follow directly from a simple intuition: once everybody resists, it is difficult to submit; once submission is common, conversions to resistance are rare. In science we speak on a positive feedback.

To demonstrate the consequences, let us select the simplest choice of two linear functions: $u(r) = a(1 - r)$, $w(r) = br$. Then there are two constant solutions: $r = 0$ (total submission) and $r = 1$ (total resistance). First solution is stable if $a > b$, second one is stable if $b > a$. In this simple case, the time-dependent solution is available

$$r(t) = \frac{r_0}{r_0 + (1 - r_0) \exp[(a - b)t]} \tag{4}$$

where r_0 is the initial value of r. As we see, the result is determined by the sign of the expression $a - b$. If it is positive, the submission prevails. If it is negative, the resistance is common.

We should add two remarks. First is that the functions $u(r)$ and $w(r)$ remain unknown. Moreover, our propositions of their linear shape can be treated as useful approximations only within some range of p. However, the qualitative character of the solution is preserved also for another choice of these functions – see the comparison in Fig. 5. Second remark appeals to the political reality. Once an individual chose the resistance, his safety will be not improved when he decides back to submit, as – sooner or later – he will be called to account by the external power. That is why it is reasonable to expect that a is always less than b. For the external power, there are two strategies: either to declare an amnesty to improve the safety of ex-opponents, or to delay the problem, keeping both constants a and b as small as possible. However, if b is already large, the second strategy is not possible and the first strategy is ineffective.

At the beginning of this section we asked the question, if – in the presence of full conflict - the development of hate can be spontaneously halted. Our results indicate, that the answer is no.

6. Conclusion

We demonstrated four schemes of simulations, intended to reflect some features of real sociological mechanisms. Three of them - prejudice, distrust and misunderstanding towards members of other communities - can contribute to the development of hate. Although they seem necessary, they are not sufficient conditions of this process. On the other hand, they are sometimes functional for a

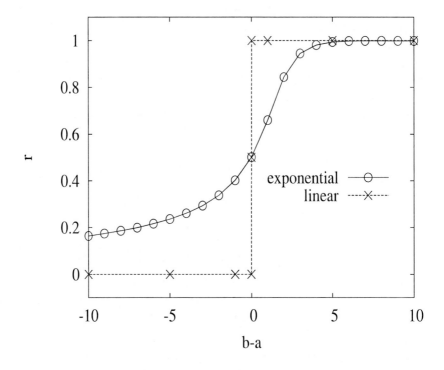

Figure 5: Stationary values of the probability r against the difference $b - a$ for linear and exponential forms of the functions $u(r)$ and $w(r)$. The exponential functions are chosen after (Kułakowski, 2006).

given community. If this is the case, the community develops social norms to support prejudice, distrust and misunderstanding, and these norms are obeyed in particular by numerous good, healthy and agreeable individuals.

The last calculation treats with the case when the hate is already present. The society is perhaps unified against the external power, perhaps split. In both cases to hate enemies is a duty and an identification. This kind of hate unifies the community; people have no choice to hate or not to hate, they have only the choice to hate whom. A demonstration of this kind of hate is equivalent to a demonstration of friendship to members of the own community. On the contrary to a private hate against a given person, this kind of hate is not destructive for the psyche. This kind of hate does not preclude friendship, sacrifice and love; it just excludes the members of hated communities.

It is not our intention here to analyze how this kind of hate turned out to be destructive for human race, even if it is still functional for some communities. Today we are educated enough to know that it is possible to live without hate; the human nature only enables hate, but does not imply it. Therefore, the research on hate should be directed more to communities and their social norms, than to rare twists of individual minds.

References

[1] Aronson, E. (1992). The Social Animal. New York: Freeman.

[2] Bickerman, E. J. (1972). The Ancient Near East, in J.A. Garraty and P. Gay (Eds.) The Columbia History of the World. New York: Harper and Row Publishers.

[3] Castellano, C., Fortunato, S., Loreto, V. (2009). Statistical physics of social dynamics. Reviews of Modern Physics 81, 591-646.

[4] Deffuant, G., Neau, D., Amblard, F., Weisbuch, G. (2000). Mixing beliefs among interacting agents. Adv. Complex Systems 3, 87-98.

[5] Fehr, E., Fischbacher, U. (2005). Human altruism – proximate patterns and evolutionary origins. Analyse und Kritik, 27, 6-47.

[6] Festinger, L. (1957). A theory of cognitive dissonance. Stanford: Stanford UP.

[7] Fortunato, F., Castellano, C. (2009). In R. A. Meyers (Ed.) Encyclopedia of Complexity and Systems Science, Vol. 1. Berlin: Springer.

[8] Fortunato, S. (2010). Community detection in graphs, Physics Reports, 486, 75-174.

[9] Freeman, L. C. (2008). Going the Wrong Way on a One-Way Street: Centrality in Physics and Biology. Journal of Social Structure, 9, No 2.

[10] Gawroński, P., Krawczyk, M. J., Kułakowski, K. (2009). Altruism and reputation: cooperation in groups, arXiv: 0903.3902.

[11] Girvan, M., Newman, M. (2002). Community structure in social and biological networks, Proc. Natl. Acad. Sci. USA 99, 7821-7826.

[12] Goette, L., Huffman, D., Meier, S. (2006). The impact of group membership on cooperation and norm enforcement: Evidence using random assignment to real social groups, working paper No. 06-7, Federal Reserve Bank of Boston.

[13] Gottman, J. M., Levenson, R. W. (1992). Marital processes predictive of latter dissolution : behavior, psychology and health. J. Personality and Social Psychol., 633, 221-233.

[14] Hage, P. (1979). Graph Theory as a Structural Model in Cultural Anthropology, Annual Review of Anthropology, 8, 115-136.

[15] Hedström, P. (2005). Dissecting the Social: On the Principles of Analytical Sociology, Cambridge: Cambridge UP.

[16] Heider, F. (1958). The Psychology of Interpersonal Relations. New York: Wiley and Sons.

[17] Helbing, D. (1993). Boltzmann-like and Boltzmann-Fokker-Planck equations as a foundation of behavioral models. Physica A, 196, 546-573.

[18] Janis, I. L. (1972). Victims of Groupthink : A psychological study of foreign-policy decisions and fiascoes. Boston: Houghton Mifflin Comp.

[19] Van Kampen, N. G. (1981). Stochastic Processes in Physics and Chemistry. Amsterdam: Elsevier.

[20] Krawczyk M. J. (2008). Differential equations as a tool for community identification. Phys. Rev. E, 77, 065701(R) 1-4.

[21] Kułakowski, K. (2007). Some recent attempts to simulate the Heider balance problem. Computing in Science and Engineering, 9, 80-85.

[22] Kułakowski, K. (2009). Opinion polarization in the Receipt-Accept-Sample model. Physica A, 388, 469-476.

[23] Kułakowski, K. (2006). Cooperation and defection in ghetto, Int. J. Mod. Phys. C 17, 287-298.

[24] Kułakowski, K., Gawroński, P. (2009). To cooperate or to defect? Altruism and reputation. Physica A, 388, 3581-3584.

[25] Kułakowski, K., Gawroński, P., Gronek, P. (2005). The Heider balance – a continuous approach. Int. J. Mod. Phys. C, 16, 707-716.

[26] Kułakowski, K., Gronek, P. (2009). The Zaller-Deffuant model of mass opinion, presented at the Dynamics Days Europe 2009, Göttingen, Aug 31 - Sept 4, 2009.

[27] Malarz, K., Gronek, P., Kułakowski, K. (2009). The Zaller-Deffuant model of public opinion, arXiv:0908.2519.

[28] Maslow, A. H. (1954). Motivation and Personality. New York: Harper.

[29] Murray, J. D. (2001). Mathematical Biology I: An Introduction. New York: Springer.

[30] Von Neumann, J., Morgenstern, O. (1944). Theory of Games and Economic Behavior. Princeton: Princeton UP.

[31] Politkovskaya, A. (2003). A Small Corner of Hell. Dispatches from Chechnya. Chicago: Univ. of Chicago Press.

[32] Roberts, G. (1998). Competitive altruism: from reciprocity to the handicap principle. Proc. R. Soc. Lond. B 265, 427-431.

[33] Sobkowicz, P., Sobkowicz, A. (2009). Dynamics of hate based networks. arXiv:0905.3751. Stauffer, D. (2004). Introduction to Statistical Physics outside Physics. Physica A, 336, 1-5.

[34] Straffin, P. D. (1993). Game Theory and Strategy. Washington, D.C.: Math. Association of America.

[35] Szabó, G., Fáth, G. (2008). Evolutionary games on graphs. Physics Reports 446, 97-216.

[36] Van Vugt, M., Roberts, G., Hardy, C. (2007). Competitive altruism: Development of reputation-based cooperation in groups, in R. Dunbar, L. Barrett, (Eds.) Handbook of Evolutionary Psychology. Oxford: Oxford University Press.

[37] Wasserman, S., Faust, K. (1994). Social Network Analysis: Methods and Applications. Cambridge: Cambridge UP.

[38] Zachary, W. W. (1977). An information flow model for conflict and fission in small groups, Journal of Anthropological Research, 33, 452-473.

[39] Zahavi, A., Zahavi, A. (1997). The Handicap Principle: The Missing Piece of Darwin's Puzzle. Oxford: Oxford University Press.

[40] Zaller, J. R. (1992). The Nature and Origins of Mass Opinion. Cambridge: Cambridge University Press.

INDEX

9

9/11, 113

A

abortion, 78
abusive, 33
acquaintance, vii, 2, 6, 7, 9, 16, 31, 69
activation, 44, 51
adaptability, 72
adaptation, 72, 124
adolescence, 56
adolescent development, 40
adolescents, 78
adults, 33, 40, 78, 92, 125, 126
aerobics, 27, 29
affective experience, 123
affective meaning, 122
affective states, 69
African-American, vii, 1, 6, 7, 9, 10, 11, 12, 13, 15, 24, 25, 27, 28, 30, 31
age, ix, 11, 36, 121, 123, 125, 142
agents, 3, 147, 148, 155
aggression, 36, 46, 52, 54, 60, 71, 72, 75, 88, 105
aggressive behavior, 78, 114
aid, 63, 87, 90
AIDS, 56
alienation, 63
altruism, 144, 145, 146, 147, 155, 157

altruistic reputation, 147
ambiguity, 72
ambivalence, 129
American culture, 40, 135
analysis of variance, 22
anger, viii, 44, 46, 50, 59, 60, 63, 65, 66, 67, 68, 71, 72, 74, 75, 76, 77, 78, 84, 87, 89, 91, 106, 123, 132
ANOVA, 16, 28
antagonistic, 41, 42
antecedents, 50, 54
antisocial personality, 134
anxiety, 69, 72, 73, 77, 78, 86, 89, 94, 97, 98, 105, 110, 111, 116, 117, 118, 123, 128, 129, 132
anxiety disorder, 78
APA, 34
application, vii, 1, 2, 3, 6, 8, 10, 11, 14, 15, 17, 19, 20, 21, 22, 27, 28, 29, 30, 31, 32, 78, 152
applications, 139, 142
argument, 30, 148
arousal, viii, 59, 71
assault, vii, 1, 2, 6, 8, 13, 14, 17, 22, 32
assaults, 5, 10
assignment, 109, 146
assimilation, 56
assumptions, 138, 147
attachment, 40, 55, 71
attacker, 30
attacks, ix, 9, 18, 21, 27, 28, 29, 42, 97, 104, 113

attempted murder, 14
attitudes, 34, 55, 57, 70, 140, 148
authority, 90, 91
autonomy, 92
aversion, 124, 132
avoidance, ix, 42, 65, 84, 117
avoidant, 55

B

barrier, x, 137, 140
behavior, viii, 7, 12, 42, 44, 45, 53, 60, 64, 65,
    68, 69, 70, 79, 112, 115, 123, 124, 128,
    129, 131, 132, 139, 152, 156
behavioral models, 156
beliefs, 41, 45, 46, 48, 57, 155
belongingness, 139, 152
benefits, viii, 35, 36, 78, 104, 135
benign, 73, 77
betrayal, 75
bias, vii, 1, 2, 3, 4, 5, 7, 8, 11, 14, 16, 17, 18,
    19, 22, 24, 25, 26, 27, 28, 29, 30, 31, 32,
    33, 34, 42, 51, 52, 56
Bible, 79, 80
blame, 66, 114
blind spot, 86, 97, 98
blocks, viii, 59, 73, 134
boys, 33
brain, 123, 124
building blocks, viii, 59, 73, 134

C

carbon, 117
caretaker, 87
catastrophes, ix, 84
catharsis, 78
cathexis, 60, 61
Caucasian, 11
causal relationship, 53
celestial bodies, 114
Chechnya, 157
childhood, 56, 91
children, 40, 106, 113

Christianity, 79
citizens, 148
civil rights, 33
clarity, 10, 85, 96
classes, viii, 11, 35, 107, 125
classification, 98
close relationships, 51
clouds, 99
clusters, 129, 142, 147
codes, 122
coding, 124
cognition, 45, 56, 57, 64, 134, 135
cognitive dissonance, 56, 141, 142, 143, 155
cognitive load, 52, 55, 57
cognitive map, 69
cognitive psychology, 122
coherence, 45, 140, 151
college students, 41
collusion, 86, 87, 88, 116, 117
colors, 134
commodity, 109
common sense, 91
communication, viii, 57, 59, 72, 98, 149, 151
communities, x, 137, 153, 155
community, x, 2, 14, 60, 137, 139, 140, 146,
    148, 151, 154, 156
competence, 92
competition, 37, 42, 89
competitors, 42
components, 45, 47, 53, 69, 124
compulsion, 71, 73
conception, ix, 5, 6, 7, 121, 123
conceptualization, 44, 45, 48, 70
conceptualizations, viii, 35
concordance, 68
conduct disorder, 78
confidence, 92, 148
conflict, viii, ix, x, 6, 30, 38, 41, 42, 49, 59,
    60, 72, 73, 84, 86, 94, 96, 98, 104, 106,
    108, 109, 110, 111, 116, 137, 140, 142,
    151, 153, 157
conflict resolution, viii, 59, 72
confusion, 25, 57, 66, 105, 115, 116
conscious awareness, 65, 68, 70
consciousness, 42, 66, 70

consensus, 138
consent, 12
constraints, 52, 53
construction, 57, 69, 97, 133
constructivism, 122
context-dependent, 50
control, 30, 38, 53, 62, 64, 72, 75, 76, 78, 93, 94, 95, 99, 109, 112, 113, 115, 139
conviction, 93
counsel, 38
counseling, 78, 79
couples, 148
courts, 85
creativity, viii, 83, 84
credit, 12, 13, 15
crime, vii, 1, 2, 3, 5, 6, 7, 8, 9, 10, 11, 14, 15, 16, 18, 20, 21, 22, 24, 26, 27, 28, 29, 30, 31, 32
criticism, 92
cross-cultural, 40
crosstalk, 47
cultivation, 77
cultural perspective, 134
cultural psychology, 55
culture, 38, 122, 135, 144
curiosity, 111
customers, 49
cycles, 85, 90, 96, 106
cycling, 111
cynicism, 72

D

danger, 73, 98
database, 33, 34
dating, 114, 122
death, 36, 88, 93, 98
debt, 64, 67, 75
decision makers, 2
decisions, 57, 152, 156
defects, 145, 147
defense, 61, 63, 65, 72, 77, 81, 86, 96, 105, 108, 118, 122
defense mechanisms, 65, 72, 122

defenses, ix, 89, 92, 96, 97, 98, 104, 110, 111, 116, 117
defensive strategies, 85
definition, viii, 3, 35, 37, 43, 44, 48, 54, 99
degrading, 22, 32
demographics, 2, 4, 5, 6, 7, 9, 10, 15, 17, 20, 24, 25, 27, 32
denial, 38, 89, 96, 108
dependent variable, 14, 16, 17, 19, 22
depressed, 91, 93, 94, 107, 109, 111, 113
depression, 66, 69, 77, 78
destruction, 37, 51, 68, 71
differentiation, viii, ix, 50, 83, 84, 87, 98, 99, 104, 111, 116
directionality, 47, 48
disability, 32, 91
disappointment, 60, 68, 109, 117
discomfort, 44, 46
discordance, 68
discourse, 37, 39, 125
discrimination, vii, 1, 3, 4, 5, 7, 8, 9, 16, 24, 26, 32, 33, 34
discriminatory, 3, 4, 5, 7, 9, 10, 11, 14, 24, 28, 29, 31, 32
disequilibrium, 71
disorder, 78
dissociation, 40
distribution, 149, 150, 151
diversity, 122
division, 118, 142, 143
divorce, 78
domestic violence, 14
dominance, 30, 94
dream, 69, 75, 95
dreams, 95
drinking, 107
drug addict, 93
duration, 75, 124

E

ecstasy, 132
education, 79
ego, viii, 59, 60, 61, 62, 65, 66, 67, 68, 70, 71, 72, 73, 74, 75, 79

ego strength, viii, 60
elaboration, 52
emotion, vii, 56, 57, 74, 75, 123, 124, 126, 134, 135
emotional, 43, 46, 63, 65, 70, 78, 85, 90, 96, 109, 113, 123, 124, 129, 132, 133, 143
emotional conflict, 109
emotional experience, 46, 123
emotional health, 78
emotional reactions, 124
emotional state, 129, 132, 133
emotions, ix, 44, 50, 60, 61, 63, 64, 68, 69, 70, 77, 121, 122, 123, 124, 131, 132, 133, 134, 135
empathy, 86
employment, 69
empowered, viii, 59, 79
empowerment, 74, 78
encouragement, 87
enemies, vii, 35, 36, 37, 38, 39, 40, 41, 42, 44, 47, 48, 49, 51, 52, 53, 54, 56, 57, 140, 141, 143, 154
energy, 60, 62, 64, 77, 78
engagement, 128
entanglements, 96, 152
entrapment, ix, 104
environment, 52, 107, 139, 143
equality, 29
equilibrium, 99, 141
ethnicity, 2
euphoria, 123, 132
evaluative conditioning, 45
evolution, 134, 143
experimental design, viii, 36
exploitation, 42
exposure, 12, 148

fear, 14, 50, 60, 63, 64, 65, 66, 68, 72, 78, 86, 88, 93, 106, 115, 116, 129, 132
fears, 85, 97, 108, 110, 117
feedback, 47, 153
feelings, ix, 42, 44, 45, 46, 48, 62, 65, 67, 68, 69, 71, 76, 77, 78, 84, 85, 86, 87, 88, 89, 92, 93, 94, 96, 97, 99, 104, 105, 108, 110, 111, 112, 115, 121, 122, 123, 124, 129
feminist, 28
fire, 27, 112
fishing, 87, 88
fission, 157
fitness, 34
fixation, 60, 71, 73, 77
flex, 89
flight, 106, 118
flow, 157
fluid, 70, 72
focusing, 48, 89
food, 111, 145, 152
football, 50
forgetting, viii, 59
forgiveness, viii, 59, 61, 62, 63, 65, 66, 67, 68, 71, 73, 74, 75, 76, 77, 78, 79, 80, 81
fragmentation, 106
free will, 139
freedom, 64, 67, 68, 75, 106, 110, 118
Freud, 60, 71, 73, 79, 123, 134
friction, 86
friendship, 39, 142, 152, 154, 155
friendship networks, 142
frustration, 42, 46, 60, 68
fuel, 77, 139
fulfillment, 132
functional analysis, 54
fusion, 114

F

factor analysis, 79
failure, 85, 94, 97, 116
faith, 74
family, 30, 78, 87, 88, 93, 107, 111, 113
family members, 107
fantasy, 61

G

game theory, 145
games, 147, 157
garbage, 111
gauge, 7, 29
gay men, 6

gender, 2, 3, 5, 6, 7, 8, 9, 10, 11, 13, 15, 16, 24, 25, 27, 28, 29, 30, 31, 32, 33, 34, 52
gender identity, 32
Ghandi, 151
gift, 60, 71, 79
girls, 29, 33, 34
glasses, 112
goals, 44, 51, 135
God, 60, 66, 67, 74, 75
government, iv, 38
grants, 38
graph, 142
greed, 14
grounding, 54
group identity, 15
group membership, 6, 8, 29, 41, 49
groups, x, 2, 5, 29, 30, 38, 45, 49, 137, 140, 141, 143, 145, 146, 147, 155, 156, 157
groupthink, 151
growth, viii, ix, 70, 71, 73, 83, 84, 87, 96, 97, 98, 99, 104, 106, 110, 111, 116, 117
guidance, 91, 107, 108
guilt, 65, 66, 69, 72, 76, 78, 86, 88, 89, 90, 93, 96, 106, 110, 116
guilty, 77, 85, 88, 94, 95, 110, 113, 118

H

H1, 11
H_2, 11
hands, 107
hanging, 89, 112
happiness, 123, 128, 129, 132
harassment, 14, 38
harm, viii, ix, 4, 5, 7, 8, 9, 10, 15, 25, 32, 33, 34, 35, 41, 44, 45, 46, 47, 48, 49, 50, 51, 52, 54, 78, 93, 104
harmony, 78
hate crime, vii, 1, 2, 3, 4, 5, 6, 7, 8, 9, 10, 11, 14, 15, 16, 19, 20, 21, 22, 23, 24, 25, 26, 27, 28, 29, 30, 31, 32, 33, 34
Hate Crime Statistics Act, 3, 34
haze, 69
healing, 62, 63, 68, 73, 75, 78, 79, 80, 89, 106, 118

health, 60, 73, 78, 80, 111, 113, 156
Heider balance, x, 137, 141, 142, 157
helplessness, 132
heroism, 138
heterogeneous, 140
high risk, 148
high school, 93, 113
hip, 54, 62, 122
Hispanic, 11
homeostasis, 73
hopes, 44, 86, 97
hospital, 13, 90
hospitalized, 13
host, 45, 47, 52
hostilities, 143
hostility, 80, 86, 140, 146, 148, 151
human, 36, 37, 45, 54, 60, 63, 64, 69, 70, 71, 72, 74, 75, 76, 77, 78, 80, 122, 123, 124, 135, 138, 139, 151, 155
human behavior, 124, 139
human development, 36, 71
human experience, 37
human nature, 36, 74, 155
human psychology, 45
humanity, 37, 74, 114
humans, vii, 36, 74
Hunter, 61, 72, 80
husband, 76, 77, 127
hypothesis, viii, 17, 18, 19, 20, 21, 27, 36, 46, 56, 125, 142
hypothesis test, viii, 17, 36, 46

I

ideal, 116, 122
identification, ix, 24, 49, 51, 84, 85, 86, 88, 89, 90, 91, 92, 95, 96, 97, 98, 99, 104, 105, 106, 108, 110, 114, 116, 117, 118, 142, 154, 156
identity, viii, 15, 32, 37, 39, 48, 51, 55, 56, 59, 70, 73, 87, 105
ideology, 41
image, 60, 61, 62, 67, 68, 69, 70, 71, 73, 74, 75, 87, 88, 89, 94

images, 40, 41, 56, 57, 69, 70, 71, 72, 75, 77, 114, 122
imaging, viii, 59
imitation, 74
in situ, 31, 139
incentives, 146
incest, 78
inclusion, 2, 3, 32
independence, 44, 110, 117
independent variable, vii, 1, 16, 17, 19, 20, 22, 27, 53
indication, 37, 42
indicators, 127
indices, 22
individual character, 139
individual differences, viii, 17, 26, 35, 52
individuality, 92
individuation, viii, ix, 83, 84, 103, 104, 105, 117
industry, 107, 108
inferences, 56
inferiority, 94
information processing, 46, 52
injury, 32, 62, 63, 64, 65, 66, 67, 76, 84, 117, 132
injustice, 63
inner tension, 60
insanity, 14
insight, 54, 97, 105
instinct, 60, 71, 75, 98
intangible, 140
integration, viii, 35, 56, 63, 66, 85, 98, 111
integrity, 65, 73
intellect, ix, 67, 121
intelligence, 91, 125, 138
intentionality, 15
intentions, 7, 74, 127
interaction, 23, 28, 31, 49, 105, 109, 150
interactions, vii, 16, 22, 25, 39, 49, 105, 140
interface, 78
internalization, 68
international relations, 41
interpersonal conflict, 36, 41
interpersonal interactions, 39, 49, 105
interpersonal relations, 36, 39, 56, 68

interpersonal relationships, 36, 39
intervention, 61, 78, 79
interview methodology, 39
intimacy, 6, 10, 14, 25, 30, 49, 50, 62, 80
intimidating, 91
introspection, 53
intuition, 152
investment, 92
IQ, 125
irritability, 72
IRS, 38
isolation, 116

J

Japanese, 38
Jerusalem, 80
Jews, 6
Jordan, 1
journalists, 38
judge, 52, 113, 114
judgment, 86, 87, 91, 99, 105, 108, 118
jurors, 24
justice, 33, 65, 66
justification, 46

K

killing, 2, 27, 115
Kleinian, 81, 84, 86, 95, 100, 101, 104, 105, 116, 119
knots, 85
Kyoto Protocol, 145

L

labeling, vii, 1, 2, 3, 4, 7, 9, 14, 16, 20, 21, 26, 27, 28, 30, 32, 140
language, 12, 125
Latinos, 6
law, 3, 62, 107
laws, 3, 32, 138, 151
lawyers, 25
leaks, 108

learning, x, 137, 140
legislation, 2, 32
lifespan, 36
lifestyle, 106
Likert scale, 14, 16
limitation, 6, 25, 31, 144
limitations, 24, 78
line, 10, 21, 23, 94, 147
linear, 153, 154
linear function, 153
links, 47, 117, 142, 143
Local Law Enforcement Hate Crimes
    Prevention Act, 3
loneliness, 63
longevity, 49
losses, 56
love, viii, ix, 30, 63, 67, 69, 71, 72, 75, 83, 84,
    87, 106, 109, 110, 114, 121, 122, 123, 124,
    125, 126, 127, 128, 129, 130, 131, 132,
    133, 134, 135, 152, 155
low risk, 148
lying, 114

M

magnetism, 152
maintenance, 54
males, 13
malicious, 42, 127
manic, 89
manipulation, 2, 8, 10, 15, 17, 22, 29, 32, 113
manners, 95
MANOVA, 22
marital status, 148
marriage, 36, 78, 127
mask, 78
mass media, 149
matrix, 142, 145, 147
meanings, 43
measurement, 48, 138, 139, 140, 148
measures, 28
media, 12, 61, 148, 149
mediation, 20, 21
memory, 44, 51, 57, 74, 91, 133

men, 2, 6, 11, 25, 27, 33, 78, 89, 90, 91, 125,
    126
mental capacity, 52, 149, 150
mental health, 78
mental representation, ix, 51, 121, 124
messages, 113, 149, 151
meta-analysis, 79
metaphors, 122
middle class, 106
minorities, 28
minority, vii, 1, 3, 5, 17, 18, 19, 27
misidentified, 16
misunderstanding, 154
mobility, 60, 71
model, x, 3, 4, 7, 8, 9, 10, 15, 17, 19, 20, 21,
    24, 25, 28, 32, 56, 80, 137, 138, 140, 142,
    147, 149, 150, 156, 157
models, 15, 20, 135, 156
mood, 78
mood disorder, 78
morning, 114
motion, 74, 78, 133
motivation, 28, 29, 45, 46, 56, 135, 145, 148
motives, 7, 8, 10, 11, 18, 26, 27, 28, 30, 32,
    41, 46
movement, 63, 66, 68
multidimensional, x, 121, 128
multidimensional scaling, x, 121, 128
multivariate, 22
murder, 14, 151
muscles, 87, 89
mutuality, 47
mythology, 38

N

narcissism, 52, 62, 123, 134
narratives, 125, 127, 128, 129
national origin, 2
natural, 62, 98, 139
Near East, 155
negative emotions, ix, 56, 68, 75, 121, 124,
    132
negative experiences, 46, 133
negative valence, 123, 124

negativity, 44
neglect, 35
network, 41
neurological disease, 91
neuropsychology, 135
nodes, 142, 143
non-violent, 7, 8
norms, 139, 154, 155

O

obese, 112
obligation, 93, 108
observations, 142
offenders, 14
openness, 66, 68, 72, 73, 75
opponent process theory, 123, 135
order, 7, 29, 40, 43, 52, 98, 99, 116, 128, 151, 152
organism, 62
organizational justice, 33
orientation, 3, 25, 71

P

pain, 45, 46, 61, 62, 65, 75, 80, 135
paradox, 75, 80
paradoxical, 55, 63, 150
parameter, 144
parents, 40, 78, 90, 106, 107
passive, viii, 42, 72, 84, 87, 90, 97, 111
patients, viii, ix, 69, 83, 84, 86, 89, 95, 96, 97, 98, 103, 104, 106, 111, 117, 118
peers, 40, 56
penis, 94
perception, viii, 5, 7, 10, 11, 15, 17, 18, 20, 22, 24, 25, 26, 27, 28, 29, 30, 31, 32, 35, 51, 52, 125, 129, 132
perceptions, 3, 5, 6, 8, 15, 25, 27, 29, 30, 31, 32, 33, 34, 47, 49, 56, 70, 124, 128
perpetrators, vii, 1, 3, 15, 16, 28, 29, 33
personal identity, 70
personal life, 70
personal relations, vii, 43, 49, 54

personal relationship, 43, 49, 54
personality, 52, 57, 68, 88, 97, 105, 123, 134, 135
philosophers, 138
philosophical, 122
physical health, 78, 80
physicists, 142
physics, 138, 139, 152, 155
physiological, 43, 124, 139, 151, 152
pilot study, 126
play, 5, 26, 52, 68, 71, 85, 98, 106
pleasure, 61, 129, 132, 135
polarization, 56, 156
police, 4, 13, 25, 33
political meeting, vii, 2, 8
political parties, 148
politicians, 38
politics, 148
poor, 69, 107
poor performance, 69
ports, 157
positive emotions, 122, 132
positive feedback, 153
posture, 118
power, 4, 14, 30, 37, 42, 62, 63, 67, 68, 71, 78, 93, 94, 112, 114, 151, 152, 153, 154
power relations, 62
pragmatic, 48
prayer, 74
preadolescents, 56
predictors, 40
prejudice, 3, 7, 8, 14, 15, 16, 17, 18, 19, 22, 26, 27, 28, 30, 31, 32, 33, 34, 143, 148, 151, 153, 154
private, 7, 96, 154
private practice, 96
proactive, 72
probability, 142, 144, 147, 149, 150, 152, 154
probability distribution, 150
program, 12, 125
protection, 86, 87, 88, 93, 123
protocol, 13
prototype, vii, 1, 3, 4, 5, 6, 7, 9, 10, 11, 15, 19, 22, 24, 25, 27, 29, 30, 32, 33, 49
provocation, 151

psyche, 155
psychic energy, 64
psychoanalysis, 80, 91, 100, 101, 118, 119, 134
psychological injury, 65, 67
psychological processes, 45
psychology, 11, 55, 56, 57, 134, 135, 156
psychopathy, 52
psychotherapy, 78, 79
psychotic, 94, 112, 113, 114
public opinion, 139, 148, 149, 157
punishment, ix, 73, 86, 88, 104
punitive, 86
Pyszczynski, 46, 56

R

race, 2, 3, 5, 6, 8, 9, 10, 11, 13, 15, 16, 25, 28, 31, 111, 155
random, x, 7, 28, 137, 140, 146, 156
range, 125, 143, 147, 153
rape, 14
rationality, 144
reading, 29, 134
reading comprehension, 134
real numbers, 143
reality, 51, 70, 72, 75, 94, 112, 125, 133, 138, 153
reason, 29, 47, 48, 49, 73, 99, 148, 152
rebelliousness, 86
recall, 77
reciprocity, 145, 157
recognition, 28, 63, 64, 133
reconciliation, viii, 47, 59, 60, 63, 65, 73, 75, 80
recurrence, 67
reflection, 106
regression, 17, 18, 19, 20, 21
regression analysis, 17, 20
regressions, 16, 22
regular, 97, 115
regulation, 124
rejection, viii, ix, 7, 30, 75, 84, 87, 94, 97, 104, 133

relationship, vii, 1, 5, 6, 7, 8, 9, 10, 15, 16, 20, 21, 25, 26, 30, 31, 32, 37, 39, 40, 42, 43, 44, 45, 47, 48, 49, 51, 53, 54, 57, 61, 62, 68, 72, 76, 78, 81, 90, 92, 96, 98, 107, 110, 122, 128, 134
relationship quality, 134
relationships, vii, 22, 35, 36, 39, 40, 42, 47, 49, 50, 51, 52, 53, 55, 62, 69, 72, 78, 79, 96, 122, 123, 124, 128, 133, 134
relatives, 107
relief, 63, 75, 106, 132
religion, 2, 5, 9, 78
religiosity, 52
religious beliefs, 74
repair, 95, 115
reparation, 74
repetitions, 122
representative samples, 38, 53
repression, 65
reputation, 147, 155, 156, 157
resentment, 67
resistance, 151, 152, 153
resolution, viii, 51, 59, 72, 90
resources, 36, 42, 52, 146
restructuring, 62, 63, 64, 78
retaliation, 7, 30, 62, 63, 66, 72, 73, 77, 80, 105
retention, 69
retribution, 44, 62, 66, 69, 73, 117
rewards, 61, 75
rhetoric, 134
righteousness, 68
risk, viii, 60, 62, 63, 65, 68, 85, 87, 148
risk-taking, viii, 60, 65, 68
robbery, 7, 14
role relationship, 96
rumination, 54

S

sabotage, 43
sadness, 68, 123, 132
safety, 62, 139, 152, 153
sample, 11, 12, 16, 25, 126
satisfaction, 60, 69, 71, 72, 132

scaling, x, 121, 128, 131, 132
schema, 3, 125, 133, 134
Schizophrenia, 119
school, 3, 14, 29, 93, 104, 106, 113, 114, 125
scientific understanding, 39
scores, 127
scripts, ix, 121, 122, 124, 125, 126, 128, 129,
     130, 131, 132, 133, 134
secondary schools, 125
secret, ix, 40, 48, 84, 88, 94, 113
security, 69
seed, 106
selecting, 10, 28
Self, 51, 56
self representation, 55
self-concept, 46, 51
self-conception, 46
self-esteem, 72
self-image, 47, 70, 73
self-interest, 64
self-worth, 73
separateness, 118
separation, viii, ix, 83, 84, 96, 98, 103, 104,
     105, 117, 139
services, 69, 111
severity, 1, 5, 8, 9, 15, 16, 19, 21, 24, 26, 31,
     32
sex, 5, 52, 91, 93, 94, 122, 134
sexism, 26
sexual abuse, 78
sexual assault, 6, 14
sexual orientation, 2, 5, 9, 25, 32
shame, 85, 94, 118, 123
shape, 152, 153
shares, 44
sharing, 36, 115
shy, 86
sibling, 38, 51
sign, 97, 153
signals, 71, 140, 148
signs, 113, 142
simulation, x, 137, 138, 140, 142, 143, 147,
     148, 149, 151, 152
simulations, x, 137, 138, 139, 140, 153
skills, 40, 107

sleep, 145
social categorization, 57
social construct, 133
social context, 135
social events, 122
social experiment, 145
social group, 156
social network, 142
social norms, 139, 154, 155
social problems, 36, 54
social psychology, 39, 54, 55, 56
social relations, 36, 42, 53, 54, 69, 122
social relationships, 36, 42, 53
social resources, 42
social sciences, 138, 139
social services, 69
social situations, 122
social skills, 40
social support, 42
social work, 69
sociological, 138, 139, 142, 150, 153
sociologists, 138, 142
sodomy, 14
Soviet Union, 57
space, 55, 114, 117
species, 36
specificity, 124
spectrum, 85, 139
speech, 8, 9, 33
spiritual, 75, 78, 79, 80
sports, 107
spouse, 51
stages, 65, 67, 122
standard error, 21, 23
standards, 5, 55, 108
state laws, 3
statutes, 2, 24
stereotypes, 54, 57
stimulus, 124
stochastic, 156
stomach, 109
strategies, 85, 125, 151, 153
strength, viii, 47, 55, 60
stress, 62, 107, 109
strokes, 42

structuring, 70
students, 11, 41, 56, 125
subjective, 36, 123, 124
subjective well-being, 36, 123
substrates, 44, 55
suffering, 44, 55, 96
suicidal, 113, 114
suicide, 2
superego, 86, 98
superiority, 61
supervisor, 69
surprise, 138
survival, 36
survivors, 56, 78
symbols, 122
symmetry, 149, 150

T

tar, 13
targets, 9
taste, 106, 114
teaching, 95
temporal, 42, 149
tension, 60, 71, 72, 73, 74, 75, 77, 78
terrorist attack, 113
therapy, 80, 111
thinking, 44, 46, 73, 93, 99, 114, 115, 117, 118
thoughts, 46, 62, 68, 69, 70, 77, 87, 104, 111, 112, 113, 124, 132, 143
threat, 46, 52, 73
threatened, 60, 62
threatening, viii, 35, 44, 46, 60, 61, 62, 73, 117
threats, 14
threshold, 9, 32, 46
tics, 139
time frame, 42
tolerance, 151
torture, 61
toxic, 86, 105
training, 146
traits, ix, 121, 123, 151

transference, ix, 84, 85, 86, 87, 88, 89, 90, 91, 92, 93, 95, 96, 97, 98, 99, 100, 101, 104, 105, 106, 107, 110, 112, 116, 117, 118
transformation, viii, 59, 61, 72, 78, 88, 96, 118, 124, 133
trauma, 114
traumatic events, 77
travel, 62
trout, 88
trust, 112, 114, 115, 117, 146
typology, 126

U

unhappiness, viii, 84
univariate, 22
universality, 38

V

valence, 123, 124, 131, 133
validation, 134
values, 21, 23, 41, 140, 147, 154
vandalism, 2, 5
variability, 50
variables, vii, 1, 2, 4, 5, 10, 11, 13, 15, 17, 20, 26, 27, 52, 53, 79, 129, 130, 131, 138
variance, 6, 22, 42
victimization, 12
victims, vii, 1, 3, 7, 8, 10, 16, 25, 28, 31, 33, 34
violence, 3, 4, 6, 9, 14, 24, 30, 32, 72
violent, 3, 4, 7, 8, 11, 12, 15, 18, 21, 24, 31, 69, 72
violent behavior, 12
violent crime, 3
visible, 33
vision, 127
visions, 122
visual perception, 55
visualization, 146
vocabulary, 122
vocational, 125
vocational schools, 125

W

wants and needs, 70
Watergate, 38
weakness, 62
wellbeing, 37, 111
well-being, 36, 55, 70, 72, 78, 123
wellness, 78
West Africa, 40, 54
Western culture, 41

women, 2, 5, 6, 7, 9, 11, 25, 27, 29, 30, 31, 33, 125, 126, 127
working-class backgrounds, 125
workplace, 4, 5, 9
worry, 88, 94

Z

Zen, 79